Cher Memoir

The 2025 Unofficial Biography of a Timeless Icon

Lena Whitmore

CBY
PRESS

Published by
CBY Press

Ordering Information:
Quantity sales: Special discounts are available on quantity purchases by corporations, associations, and others. For details, reach out to the publisher.

First published by CBY Press, 2025

Contents

TIMELINE

1946	Cherilyn Sarkisian (Cher) is born on May 20 in El Centro, California.
1962	Drops out of high school and moves to Los Angeles to pursue her dreams.
1963	Meets Sonny Bono, who becomes her mentor and partner.
1965	Sonny & Cher release "I Got You Babe," which becomes a massive hit.
1965	Releases her first solo album, All I Really Want to Do.
1967	Sonny & Cher's film Good Times is released but fails commercially.
1969	Gives birth to her daughter, Chastity Bono (later Chaz Bono).
1971	The Sonny & Cher Comedy Hour debuts on CBS and becomes a hit.
1971	Releases her solo album Gypsys, Tramps & Thieves, featuring the chart-topping title track.
1972	Wins a Golden Globe for Best Actress in a Television Series for The Sonny & Cher Comedy Hour.
1974	Divorces Sonny Bono after marital and professional tensions.
1975	Marries Gregg Allman but files for divorce after just nine days; reconciles briefly.
1976	The Sonny & Cher Show debuts, attempting to revive their TV success post-divorce.
1979	Returns to music with the disco album Take Me Home, marking her comeback.
1982	Makes her Broadway debut in Come Back to the 5 & Dime, Jimmy Dean, Jimmy Dean.
1983	Receives critical acclaim for her role in the film Silkwood, earning an Academy Award nomination.
1987	Wins an Academy Award for Best Actress for her performance in Moonstruck.

1989	Releases the hit single "If I Could Turn Back Time" from the album Heart of Stone.
1996	Stars in the HBO film If These Walls Could Talk, tackling the topic of abortion rights.
1998	Suffers the loss of her ex-husband Sonny Bono in a skiing accident.
1998	Releases Believe, which introduces Auto-Tune as a vocal effect and becomes a global hit.
1999	Wins her first Grammy Award for Best Dance Recording for "Believe."
2000	Begins her Farewell Tour, which lasts for three years due to its immense popularity.
2002	Releases Living Proof, her 25th studio album.
2008	Begins a residency at Caesars Palace in Las Vegas, titled Cher at the Colosseum.
2010	Appears in the musical film Burlesque alongside Christina Aguilera.
2013	Releases her album Closer to the Truth, her first in over a decade.
2018	Stars in Mamma Mia! Here We Go Again and releases a covers album, Dancing Queen.
2020	Advocates for political and social causes, including LGBTQ+ rights and the environment.
2023	Continues to perform music and remain a cultural icon across multiple generations.

PREFACE: MEETING ELVIS

As Cher's mother and she sat on the couch watching The Ed Sullivan Show, the television screen came alive with the electrifying presence of a young Elvis Presley. It was September 1956, and they were among the millions of Americans witnessing what would become a historic performance. That evening, Elvis, though conservatively dressed, moved and sang in a way that captivated Cher entirely. His rendition of "Don't Be Cruel" transitioned seamlessly into "Love Me Tender," and she felt as if his gaze pierced through the screen, speaking only to her.

A year later, news spread that Elvis would perform at the Pan-Pacific Auditorium in Los Angeles. Cher, then an exuberant eleven-year-old, ran home bursting with excitement. "Mom, Elvis is coming to the Pan-Pacific! Can we go? Please?" Her voice was filled with urgency and hope, certain that she had to be there. Deep down, she imagined that, somehow, he might notice her in the sea of faces and single her out–though she suspected every girl had the same fantasy.

Fortune smiled upon Cher that day. Her mother, Georgia, shared her adoration for Elvis, which set her apart from the other mothers who frowned upon his daring charm. Despite tight finances, Georgia found a way to make it happen. On the night of the concert, the two dressed up, looking more like sisters than mother and daughter. Excitement grew as they approached the Fairfax District, and soon they were swept into a massive, energetic crowd of fans buzzing with anticipation.

Inside the Pan-Pacific, the atmosphere was electric. Their seats, though not at the front, offered a clear view of the stage. Cher's heart raced in a way that would later become familiar in her life, her chest pounding with excitement as she joined the throng of nine thousand screaming fans. When the lights dimmed and the spotlight hit Elvis, the auditorium erupted in a roar unlike anything Cher had ever experienced.

Elvis stood there, dazzling in a golden suit that shimmered under the lights. His charisma was palpable, his smile captivating, and his jet-black hair a striking match for Cher's own. As the crowd erupted into a frenzy, Cher joined the chorus of screams. The sound of "Heartbreak Hotel" was nearly drowned out by the chaos, but Elvis's signature moves–his swiveling hips and quivering legs–were impossible to miss. Girls climbed onto their seats, obstructing the view, leaving only glimpses of his head and shoulders visible.

Amid the pandemonium, Cher found herself swept up in the hysteria, though she didn't fully understand the magnitude of what was happening. If she had been older, perhaps, the raw energy of the moment might have struck her differently. Still, it was a night of pure magic. Watching Elvis in his element planted a dream deep within her—a vision of herself on a stage, bathed in the spotlight, performing with the same hypnotic power.

Glancing over at her mother, Cher saw that Georgia was equally mesmerized, her elegance standing out even in the chaos. For a fleeting moment, Cher was convinced Elvis might notice her mom instead. Pressing close to her mother's ear, she shouted above the noise, "Mom, can we stand on our seats and scream too?"

Georgia laughed, slipping off her heels. "Of course! Let's do it!" Together, they climbed onto their chairs, straining to see Elvis through the sea of waving arms and flashing cameras.

In that golden moment, Cher's imagination soared. She wondered if Elvis would still be young enough to marry her by the time she was grown, dreaming of a life where he would serenade her every day. For weeks after the concert, she floated on a cloud of excitement, unable to stop talking about the experience. Elvis had not only captured her heart but ignited a fire within her—a desire to one day create magic of her own on the stage.

CHAPTER 1

ROOTS OF RESILIENCE

THE MOTHER AS A CHILD

During the Great Depression, Cher's grandparents managed to survive thanks to government aid–basic supplies like beans, flour, lard, and canned milk. Her grandmother spent hours in line to secure these essentials. It was a time of immense hardship, marked by malnutrition and illness that claimed countless lives.

When he was young, Cher's grandfather Roy dreamed of outlaw fame. But he fell for twelve-year-old Lynda, a naïve farm girl, who became pregnant after a moonlit swim. At thirteen, Lyndra was too young to handle motherhood.

Roy turned to moonshine and other women, perpetuating cycles of violence by beating his wife. Arrested over thirty times, Roy went on the run after attacking a sheriff, dragging his young family into a life of labor and poverty. Baby Jackie Jean's earliest memory was riding in a cotton sack as her mum worked under the sun, their meals often just biscuits and molasses or a rabbit if lucky.

Jackie Jean was a sickly child, plagued by ailments like rheumatic fever and strep throat, which her grandmother Margaret treated with home remedies. When Jackie fell seriously ill with German measles, her struggling parents couldn't afford a doctor and handed her over to the Salvation Army until she recovered.

Despite these early challenges, Jackie grew into a striking child with a voice that stunned anyone who heard her. Roy lovingly nicknamed her "Jack" and often swelled with pride at her singing. Lynda was still in her teens and didn't take naturally to motherhood, leaving Jackie to pour her affection into her father, who was caring and fun–when sober. Roy took her everywhere, including speakeasies, where he'd lift her onto the bar to sing while he drank.

One night at the Shamrock Saloon in Saint Louis, Roy passed a hat around after Jackie's performance and was astonished to collect sixteen cents. With the change, he bought liquor and handed the rest to Jackie, who ran to the store to buy groceries, including sweet tea ingredients for her mother. From that moment, Roy saw Jackie's talent as a way to make ends meet, and she became the family's breadwinner.. Crowds loved her, tossing coins her way until her pockets sagged from the weight.

Lynda, jealous of the attention Jackie received and tired of Roy's neglect, eventually left without warning and left Jackie behind. Roy's life spiraled further. He moved Jackie into the care of his sister Lodema, where Jackie was molested by her uncle. She confided in her aunt, who silenced her with carbolic soap. Singing "Danny Boy" with Roy, Jackie Jean found solace. "I could fly away from the trouble and the pain.

The father-daughter duo eventually left Saint Louis for Oklahoma City, where Jackie performed on WKY radio and sang with local bands. "You're really going to be somebody," he said with conviction Her voice caught the attention of Bob Wills, a popular musician, who predicted her talent would bring fame. Roy, fueled by these words, dragged Jackie to every bar in town, where she performed barefoot on counters until they earned enough for food and liquor. She would never forget the stink of the bars, though.

When Prohibition ended, Roy briefly reunited with Lynda, who returned long enough to have another child. The family struggled to make ends meet, surviving on scraps and goodwill. Desperate for a breakthrough, Roy decided to take Jackie to Hollywood, convinced she could become the next Shirley Temple. The winter of 1934 saw the pair hitchhiking west, enduring hunger and harsh conditions along the way. A kind couple bought Jackie her first coat, and a bus driver ferried them part of the journey for free.

JACKIE'S JOURNEY

In Los Angeles, Even more disheartening was how everyone mocked them, ridiculing their accents and tattered clothes by calling them "dumb Okies." But she'd learnt that survival meant summoning the strength to keep moving forward, no matter what. Despite her poverty, she carried herself with the dignity and poise of a queen.

Roy, clueless about navigating Hollywood, took a job as a baker, while Jackie won local talent contests and performed on the radio. Despite her successes, financial struggles prevented her from seizing larger opportunities, like joining the Meglin Kiddies troupe.

When Roy's efforts to build a stable life faltered, he sent Jackie back to Arkansas to live with his sister Zella. Those six months were some of Jackie's happiest, as she was finally cared for and valued. But when she learned Lynda had abandoned her little brother Mickey, Jackie returned to protect him.

The reunion with her family in Oklahoma City brought new hardships, including the worst night of Jackie's life. The details fragmented memory were uncovered only through therapy years later. They were staying in a filthy place crawling with biting insects. She forced herself to stay awake out of fear that men might break in and harm her and Mickey. But exhaustion took over, and she awoke to the sound of hissing.

Half-asleep, she imagined the room was full of snakes before realizing the noise was gas. A shadowy figure crossed the room, and she feigned sleep until he left. Choking, she grabbed Mickey and ran to a neighbor, who called the police. Later, she realized the figure was her father, Roy. Sober and deliberate, he had come home, turned on the gas, and walked away. For years, she struggled to accept that the only parent who seemed to love her had tried to end her life.

Life eventually led Jackie and her family to Los Angeles, where her Sicilian stepfather treated her with kindness, giving her the nickname "String Bean." Yet, even this period of relative stability didn't last. When her mother left again, Jackie, at thirteen, decided to take control of her own life. She found work as a live-in maid, balancing her duties with school. Despite her challenging circumstances, Jackie excelled academically and worked tirelessly to refine her accent and hone her talent.

By the time she was fifteen, Jackie's dreams of college were cut short when Roy, injured and in need of care, begged her to return to Oklahoma. Out of a mix of love and duty, she went back, though she resolved to one day return to Los Angeles, the city she now saw as her true home.

That decision would not only shape Jackie's destiny but lay the foundation for Cher's extraordinary journey.

BEING BORN

By the time Jackie Jean turned eighteen, she was a striking young woman with an air of effortless glamour. Her thrift-store wardrobe belied her impeccable style, and her chestnut hair framed a face that could have belonged to a movie star. On the outside, she seemed poised and confident, but beneath the surface, she was still a naive small-town girl, vulnerable to the influences around her.

Raised in a strict Baptist household, her father had drilled a single message into her: no man should touch her before marriage. Those words echoed in her mind, shaping her beliefs about relationships and intimacy. After enduring a traumatic childhood experience, she resolved to save herself for "Mr. Right." But when she met a smooth-talking young man at a big band dance in Fresno, California, her resolve was put to the test. Johnnie Sarkisian wasn't her usual type—flashy clothes, too short for her liking—but there was something magnetic about him. When her blouse got caught on his shirt button during a jitterbug, she couldn't help but laugh, noticing his charm as he freed her.

Their relationship quickly progressed. It was wartime, and everything felt heightened, spontaneous, and uncertain. He taught her to drive, promised her his car, and charmed her with grand gestures. Despite her instincts, she found herself drawn to him, though she refused to cross certain boundaries. One night at the club where she sang and waited tables, someone dared him to marry her. Without much thought, he convinced her to elope to Reno, and in a whirlwind double wedding, she became his wife. Standing there, barely nineteen, she couldn't shake the feeling of unease, fighting back tears even as she said, "I do." Less than a day later, still a virgin, she fled back home, determined to annul the marriage.

Her new husband wasn't ready to let her go. He followed her, pleading for another chance. "How do you know you don't want this? You haven't even tried," he argued. Against her better judgment, she gave in. She didn't love him, but his persistence wore her down. She returned, feeling trapped in a society where women had few options. It wasn't long before their chaotic life together began—moving from place to place, relying on her income, and staying with his relatives until their welcome wore thin. While some in his family disapproved of their union, one relative, a spirited and modern woman, embraced her fully, becoming her only ally in an otherwise isolating situation.

The marriage unraveled quickly. Miserable and pregnant, she found no solace from her own mother, who reacted with anger rather than compassion. Under pressure, she agreed to an illegal procedure but panicked at the last moment. Overwhelmed by fear, she left the clinic, determined to have the child. Her decision created a rift with her family, but she returned to her husband, resolved to face whatever came next. With no steady income, they moved to a small town near the Mexican border, where he tried running a trucking business. For a brief time, things seemed stable, but his late-night poker games and absence from home soon took a toll.

When the time came, she went into labor a month early. Exhausted and alone in a small hospital, she gave birth to a premature baby girl in May 1946. Her mother, despite their estrangement, had a change of heart and arrived just in time to welcome the new arrival, claiming to have foreseen the birth in a dream. Cher's mother was asked by a nurse what she planned to name her baby. Caught off guard, she took inspiration from her favorite actress Lana Turner's daughter, Cheryl, and her own mother, Lynda, to come up with the name Cherilyn. Cher believed this was her official name until years later, when she applied for her birth certificate and discovered it listed her as Cheryl. Confused, she asked her mother about the discrepancy. Her mother was surprised, but then simply shrugged and said, "I was a teenager and in a lot of pain—cut me some slack."

THE FLASH AND THE FALLOUT

Johnnie celebrated the birth of his daughter by gifting Jackie a ruby and diamond watch in pink gold and providing a cradle and buggy. Jackie embraced motherhood, embroidering the tiny kimono the hospital sent her baby home in. However, their modest happiness was short-lived. Six months after the birth, Johnnie admitted he had lost his father's trucking business in a card game. Their livelihood was gone.

Forced to pawn her watch, Jackie moved with her baby into a stifling steel Quonset hut in the desert. Desperate to escape, she reluctantly agreed to Johnnie's plan to move to New York, where his sister might fund his next scheme. After a grueling fifty-hour bus ride, Johnnie revealed he had stolen a car and sold it in Mexico to pay for the trip. Baby Cher cried constantly and Jackie tried in vain to soothe her. She later summed up her feelings about that phase of her life. "I didn't do well as a mother. I was too hysterical from stress."

In New York, Johnnie's sister Liz had no money or space to help them. Jackie, bundled in Johnnie's overcoat, wandered the freezing streets with her infant pressed to her chest. With Johnnie too paranoid to work, she found a job as a cigarette girl at the Copacabana nightclub, where she impressed her mobster boss. Though the tips were good, Johnnie's fears of police drove them to leave abruptly.

They relocated to Scranton, Pennsylvania, where Johnnie's promises of work proved empty. Desperate, Jackie urged him to take action. Johnnie persuaded a priest to temporarily place their daughter in a Catholic children's home, vowing to return in two weeks. Alone in a cramped room after long shifts, Jackie cried herself to sleep. She visited her baby twice a week, her only solace amidst the hardship.

Just as stability seemed possible, Jackie discovered she was pregnant again—with Johnnie's child, the only man she had ever been with. She turned to Dave, a married City Council member and regular customer who tipped generously when she sang "My Man." Begging for his help, Dave reluctantly agreed, arranging a secret abortion. The procedure left Jackie in excruciating pain, but Dave ensured she was cared for by a nurse. When she asked what would have happened if she had died, his chilling response was, "We'd have dumped your body in the river."

Weeks later, Jackie went to the children's home to see her daughter, only to be forbidden from holding her. Through a small window, she saw her baby standing in a crib, crying. Jackie broke down in tears as the nuns, critical of her Baptist background and nightclub job, deemed her an unfit mother and suggested adoption.

Desperate, Jackie pleaded with Dave again. Though he admitted he couldn't challenge the Catholic Church, he confronted the nuns, demanding they release the child. Intimidated, they relented, and Jackie finally reclaimed her daughter, who had gone from crawling to walking during their separation.

The trauma lingered for years. Decades later, Cher reflected on the pain in her song "Sisters of Mercy," giving Jackie a sense of vindication and a voice for their shared struggles.

CHAPTER 2

GLAMOR AND CHAOS

A LIFE OF UNCERTAINTY

Cher's childhood was far from normal, shaped by abandonment and upheaval. After rescuing her baby from the nuns, Jackie Jean traveled to Twin Falls, Idaho, where her father Roy and younger brother Mickey lived in squalor. Taking Mickey with her, she moved to Los Angeles, leaving Cher in the care of her grandmother Lynda while she worked as a waitress to make ends meet. Jackie relied on Lynda's friends, Mackie and Edith, to babysit Cher. Years later, during a performance in Las Vegas, Cher met Mackie, who revealed she had cared for her when she was little. Mackie even brought a worn highchair that had once been Cher's, leaving her stunned to learn she had lived with strangers for much of her early life.

"Where was Mom all this time?" Cher asked Lynda later, piecing together fragmented memories.

Lynda hesitated before admitting Jackie had left Cher while pursuing a new life in Reno, Nevada. Pressured by her mother, Jackie entered a beauty pageant and was crowned "Model Miss," catching the eye of millionaire Ernest Primm. Lynda, obsessed with finding her daughter a wealthy husband, encouraged the relationship. Ernie, enchanted by Jackie's elegance and talent, showered her with gifts and refined her manners, promising a life of luxury–on one condition: Cher could not be part of the deal.

Jackie, dazzled by Ernie's wealth and guided by Lynda's advice, postponed her own dreams, leaving Cher with Mackie and Edith while she waited for Ernie's divorce to finalize. This marked another chapter of abandonment in Cher's life, one that left a lasting impact on her sense of self.

A WORLD OF LOVE, LOSS, AND STARDOM

A LIFE IN DRAMA: NEW BEGINNINGS AND THE LOVE THAT SHAPED ME

At a Hollywood gala, Jackie Jean met the tall, handsome Chris Alcaide. After secretly dating him behind her fiancé Ernie's back, Jackie knew she had to choose. Chris's warmth toward her young daughter sealed the deal. She left Ernie, giving up security and wealth, and married

Chris, making him her second husband. Their life together included Jackie's enrollment in Ben Bard's drama school, where she trained alongside future stars like Rod Steiger and Robert Mitchum. Jackie thrived in her acting classes, booking commercials and performing in musicals. Her daughter often tagged along, enchanted by the world of theater and memorizing Shakespeare at just four years old.

However, Chris's jealousy and drinking eventually escalated into violence. One night, after a tipsy actor flirted with Jackie at a party, Chris's simmering anger boiled over. He shoved Jackie against the wall, his hands tightening around her throat. Desperation took over, and she shouted, "What will happen to Cher if you kill me and end up in jail?" His drunken rage faltered, and it was his care for Cher that made him stop. Jackie left him soon after. Following her divorce, she briefly considered reuniting with Ernie, but when he insisted Cher wouldn't live with them, she ended it for good.

Jackie soon met E.J. "John" Southall, a Texan actor and former B-29 captain. Their love was instant and profound. John became her third husband and the first man to truly step into the role of fatherhood for her daughter. With charm, good looks, and a deep love for his new family, John offered stability, even as he pursued acting alongside his door-to-door aluminum siding job. Jackie, now a dedicated actor, took small roles in *Gunsmoke*, *I Love Lucy*, and other shows. She admired Lucille Ball but had to navigate inappropriate advances from both Desi Arnaz and Ozzie Nelson.

John's love and Jackie's relentless determination defined their unconventional family. Surrounded by actors, artists, and dreamers, Jackie taught her daughter resilience and creativity, shaping the vibrant world she called home. Through her struggles and triumphs, Jackie remained a fearless and loving mother.

A STAR IN THE MAKING

Cher's childhood was a mix of vivid imagination and emotional highs and lows, shaped by At five, Cher was already developing her imagination and personality in ways that would shape her life. Living in Laurel Canyon, her family resided among artists, bohemians, and musicians in a vibrant but modest community. Their funky home on Lookout Mountain was filled with both challenges and creativity. Cher's babysitter, Maria, was tasked with distracting her from the distress of her parents going out at night. But the fear of abandonment overwhelmed Cher, resulting in dramatic tantrums. Despite her young age, she sometimes questioned herself: *What am I doing? They're just going to dinner.*

During the day, Cher's adventurous spirit took over. One afternoon, playing hide-and-seek with Maria, Cher wandered too far into the woods. Lost and scared, she called out for Maria, her imagination conjuring lurking coyotes and mountain lions. Maria found her after what felt like an eternity, comforting the frightened child. It was moments like these that led Cher to retreat into her imagination. She invented invisible friends, Sam and Pete, two lumberjack-like figures who lived under her grandparents' lemon tree. These imaginary companions became confidants, filling the loneliness that came with her parents' demanding schedules. Mamaw, her grandmother, understood Cher's need for them and reassured her mother, saying, "She's just a child–an only child. It's just a phase."

Cher's vivid imagination wasn't limited to creating friends. She believed she was an angel sent to cure polio, a disease she saw on news bulletins. When Jonas Salk invented the vaccine, she was upset, feeling her mission had been taken. Later, a half-asleep vision of Jesus in her bedroom curtains sparked dreams of sainthood, though her "chance" to become Saint Cher remained unfulfilled.

Music became another sanctuary. Singing with her mother at home or with her grandfather Roy during his annual visits, Cher developed a love for country music, especially the songs of Hank Williams. Her grandfather, weakened by years of alcoholism, still played guitar with a vibrant passion, passing down songs like "Hey, Good Lookin'" and "Your Cheatin' Heart."

Movies also played a formative role. Cher's parents took her to Grauman's Chinese Theatre to see *Dumbo*, a magical experience that left her awestruck. The grandeur of the theater, the vibrant colors on the screen, and the emotional story of the baby elephant with oversized ears captivated her. She felt so connected to Dumbo's journey that she refused to leave her seat, even when she desperately needed the bathroom. "I want to be Dumbo when I grow up," she declared afterward. Her mother gently explained that Dumbo wasn't real, but Cher's determination to be part of that magical world remained.

Her next movie, *Cinderella*, further ignited her dreams. This time, Cher decided she'd become Cinderella, inspired by the character's songs and transformation. Singing "A Dream Is a Wish Your Heart Makes" all the way home, her mother proudly pointed out her talent. "Do you hear this child? I told you she was special," she said to John.

Even as a young girl, Cher's dreams and creative energy hinted at the extraordinary path she would follow. From losing herself in imaginary worlds to finding joy in music and movies, she was already shaping the unique persona the world would one day know.

FAMILY ON THE MOVE

To save on babysitters, Jackie and John took Cher everywhere. One favorite spot was the Original Spanish Kitchen on Beverly Boulevard, a faded adobe building with a giant mural of a flamenco dancer. Cher was mesmerized by the dancer, real or imagined, spinning in her ruffled skirt. "I want to take dance lessons," she begged her parents, but they couldn't afford it. Her love for dancing, though, became a part of her soul.

On weekends, the family visited Cap's Place near Malibu. To get there, they crossed a wobbly rope bridge that thrilled Cher. Cap, a sailor resembling Popeye, let Cher sneak sips of Brew 102, which made the adults laugh.

The 1950s brought cocktail parties to their home, where actors filled the air with smoke and laughter. Cher sat quietly in the corner, hoping not to be sent to bed. The glamorous women of the group became her role models–Jake, Viv, Evelyn, and the striking red-haired actress Kathryn Reed. "These women were my life coaches," Cher said, soaking up their style, charm, and confidence.

Jackie, though, was the most beautiful. Cher vividly remembered her mother in a pale blue chiffon cocktail dress with moonstone chandelier earrings. She'd sneak the earrings to play with, dreaming of wearing them. Years later, Jackie gifted them to Cher, who nearly cried with happiness.

John was loving, playful, and stylish, letting Cher sit on his lap to steer the car. "I'll buy you wheels someday," he'd promise. But when he drank too much, his temper surfaced, leaving Cher uneasy.

Despite the chaos and arguments, Cher relished their unconventional life. "Let's never be like other people," she pleaded with Jackie. Jackie, always spontaneous, made sure life stayed exciting, from skipping school for beach trips to whispering ghost stories under the stars. Jackie and Cher sang loud, silly songs together in the car, drawing stares from strangers.

When money was tight, they'd move into cheap San Fernando Valley apartments, far from their Hollywood friends. Cher hated it there, associating the Valley with harder times, despite its excellent hamburger stands. "This isn't where I belong," she'd think, even as a little girl.

When work picked up, they'd rush back to Hollywood, where Jackie loved to dress Cher in her best dress and Mary Janes for trips to the Broadway department store on Hollywood Boulevard. They'd buy hot dogs and sit in the car, with Jackie spinning stories about the passersby. "See that man in blue? He's a magician," she'd say, or, "Look at her cheekbones. She could be the next Joan Crawford." Jackie herself looked every bit the movie star, once stopped by a stranger who exclaimed, "You *must* be a star!"

During harder times, they'd leave California entirely. At five, Cher found herself in Galveston, Texas, where John got a job. She was enrolled in school and played on the beach while Jackie sunbathed. Cher feared the ocean after a wave flipped her once, but Texas felt happy and safe. Still, the family didn't stay long, soon moving to Burleson, a small town where Cher slept in a kitchen alcove and bathed in a tin washtub. Despite scorpions, rattlesnakes, and tangled hair-washing sessions, Cher grew to love Burleson.

One day, Jackie packed up and drove back to LA, leaving John behind. A strange man in the car puzzled Cher with the way he behaved around her mother. She later told John, sparking a fight that nearly ended the marriage. Years later, Cher returned to Burleson, astonished when an old man recognized her, not as Cher the star, but as the girl who once lived in that tiny town.

THE BUTTON BOX AND THE MOVIES

One of Cher's happiest memories was getting their first TV. Jackie had a doctor's appointment, and John promised a surprise afterward. Cher assumed it would be ice cream. Instead, John took them to an appliance store, revealing a maple console television. "It's huge!" Cher thought, though it probably wasn't. Jackie was ecstatic as they brought it home, where John and Kenny set it up. "It's like a new baby," everyone marveled, but Cher's excitement dimmed when John insisted she nap before their first movie night. Restless, she sat at the window until John finally let her join them. They all gathered to watch *One Million B.C.*, and Victor Mature, with his brooding looks, became Cher's first movie crush. "Well, of course you like him," Jackie teased, though Cher didn't understand why until much later.

Between her childhood and teen years, Cher's dreams of becoming an actress grew stronger, fueled by nights spent with her mother curled up in bed with a bowl of popcorn. These evenings became their special time together. Back then, movies weren't something you chose–they simply aired–but Cher loved them all. Her mother would share

Hollywood gossip and stories about the actors and actresses, sparking Cher's fascination. Her mother's passion for singing and movies became hers as well. Yet, it was clear her mother enjoyed watching Cher's reactions even more than the films. Classics like *Gilda* with Rita Hayworth or *Gaslight* with Ingrid Bergman filled their evenings. Cher admired Hedy Lamarr in *Samson and Delilah*, while her mother adored Lana Turner, her idol, even going so far as to dye her hair blonde to resemble her. One of Cher's favorite films was *Homecoming*, in which Lana Turner played a character named Snapshot. Decades later, when Cher watched the film again, she felt an unexplained connection to it until she remembered seeing it as a child with her mother.

The movie that left the greatest impression on Cher was *The Enchanted Cottage*, starring Dorothy McGuire and Robert Young. It told the story of a disfigured war veteran and a plain woman who, through the magic of love and the cottage, saw each other as beautiful. The film's message—that beauty is in the eye of the beholder—stuck with Cher throughout her life and even influenced a movie she acted in years later. She dreamed of remaking it someday.

With both her parents working, babysitting duties often fell to Mamaw and Pa. Their relationship was old-fashioned. Mamaw would prepare Pa's bacon, eggs, biscuits, and freshly squeezed orange juice every morning, no matter how ill she felt. It was expected, though they had a quiet love for one another.

Mamaw was an extraordinary seamstress who worked at the Mildred Moore couture store in Beverly Hills. She transformed the finest fabrics into elegant outfits for herself, Cher's mother, and Cher. As a child, Cher loved sitting under Mamaw's Singer sewing machine, surrounded by velvets and silks, playing with her large button box filled with rhinestones, sequins, and mother-of-pearl treasures. "I'm trusting you with these, Cher. Don't lose any," Mamaw would say, sparking Cher's lifelong love of shiny things. Even now, that button box remains one of Cher's most cherished possessions. And no matter how real Sam and Pete, her imaginary lumberjack friends, seemed to her, they were strictly forbidden from going anywhere near it.

CHAPTER 3

GROWING PAINS

A NEW SISTER AND A NEW REALITY

By 1949, Jackie Jean had transformed into Georgia Pelham, a name inspired by her late best friend, Ann, from Pelham, Georgia. With her new name and dyed hair, she pursued her dream of stardom, but her refusal to compromise her integrity–declining advances from powerful men like Howard Hughes–cost her big roles. “I could have had my own show if I’d just laid on his couch,” she’d lament.

The biggest heartbreak came when Georgia landed a role in *The Asphalt Jungle*, only to be replaced by an unknown actress named Marilyn Monroe. “Son of a gun,” she muttered, her disappointment evident. Soon after, she discovered she was pregnant, and life shifted yet again.

With John between jobs, the family moved back in with Mamaw and Pa. Cher, thrilled about the new baby, momentarily forgot her yearning for a $6 Tiny Tears doll. Her excitement waned when her silky black hair was accidentally burned during a perm. Looking in the mirror at her frizzy poodle cut, she burst into tears.

In September 1951, the baby, Georganne–or “Gee”–was born. Cher’s initial excitement turned to frustration as everyone fawned over her sister. “I don’t see what’s so great about that baby,” John said, sitting beside Cher. “She doesn’t do anything but cry. But I guess we’ll keep her and see how she turns out.” His words made Cher feel understood. “Let’s go get ice cream,” he added, cementing her sense of belonging.

That Christmas, a surprise box appeared under the tree, marked for Cher. Inside was a stuffed yellow cat with button eyes. It became her most cherished possession, a bright spot in a season of change. Despite her struggles, Cher began to accept her new role as a big sister, thanks to her father’s unwavering love and support.

A MOTHER’S GRIT

Finding work as an actress without an agent in Hollywood was a relentless uphill battle. After long days on set, Cher’s mother, exhausted but determined, would collapse onto the couch with her favorite soda, Dr Pepper, and begin the nightly ritual of calling casting directors. Cher would watch as her mother spun the dial phone for hours, her persistence unyielding as she pleaded for extra roles. Casting directors admired her beauty, but that often worked against her; she could never outshine the leading actress. Still, she kept trying, knowing that one phone call could mean a meal on the table and a chance to stay afloat.

At dawn, she would rise and meticulously apply her makeup for whatever small role she'd secured the night before. Hollywood in the 1950s wasn't kind to women, and her mother carried the weight of their survival alone. Without support from Cher's biological father, Johnnie, and with few reliable men in her life, every burden fell squarely on her shoulders. Often, she skipped meals at work, sipping a Coke instead of joining the other actors, too broke to buy lunch. At five feet seven inches, she weighed barely more than a hundred pounds, the stress carving deep lines into her spirit.

Cher could feel that tension in the air, the anxiety of a mother constantly on the brink. "Cher, how on earth are we going to pay the rent?" her mother once asked, breaking down in front of her. Cher, barely more than a child, thought helplessly, *I'm just a kid, Mom. How should I know?*

Her mother's resilience shone in moments of necessity. One day, Cher came home from school to find her up on the roof, hammer in hand, nails clenched between her teeth, replacing shingles because she couldn't afford to hire help. It filled Cher with pride, even as their vagabond lifestyle left her longing for stability.

The rare periods when her parents reunited offered brief reprieves. With her father home, life became easier, safer. Cher felt the warmth of protection and routine, but those moments were fleeting. She learned early that adults were unpredictable, that vigilance was her only constant companion. While she admired her mother's strength, Cher wished for just a touch of normalcy, a fleeting glimpse of what a stable childhood might have been.

A CHILDHOOD OF CONTRASTS

In Georganne's first year, happiness surrounded the family, but their father's drinking loomed like a dark cloud. When sober, he was kind and attentive, but alcohol turned him into someone unrecognizable. Cher, just a child, learned to distract him with innocent tricks, like asking him to play in the yard. If that failed, she would quietly slip away, retreating to her room, trembling as her parents' arguments escalated into screaming matches.

One evening, the family attended a lavish Hawaiian-themed party hosted by Betty Martin in her sprawling Holmby Hills mansion. Cher was entranced by the house, marveling at its two staircases and the grand atmosphere. While she played upstairs with Betty's daughters, chaos brewed below. Her father, enraged by a perceived slight, grabbed her mother by the hair and dragged her across the tiled floor. Guests stood frozen, their silence deafening. Betty, a petite but fierce woman, confronted him. She jabbed a finger into his chest and shouted, "Hey! Nobody behaves like that in my house. Now get the hell out!"

Mortified, Cher's mother stayed behind with her children, finding refuge in a room Betty prepared for them. The next morning, Cher played with Betty's daughters, who introduced her to a family across the street. As they stepped into the home, Cher spotted a petite woman halfway up the stairs, stylish in capri pants and a patterned ensemble. The woman paused her yelling, noticed the children, and ushered them outside. Moments later, her daughter, Liza, burst into an impromptu rendition of "Somewhere Over the Rainbow." Cher found it peculiar but impressive. Only later did she realize the woman was Judy Garland, and the singing girl was Liza Minnelli.

Cher's mother often left her father during difficult times, packing the children into the car and declaring, "Anything is better than this!" Each departure came with financial struggles, forcing them to move and start over. These upheavals taught Cher survival skills but also made her hyper-aware of others' emotions, a habit that lingered throughout her life. Photos from her childhood captured her shifting moods–scowling in one moment, striking a movie-star pose in the next. It was a reflection of her emotional world, shaped by the chaos and contrasts of her early years.

Cher's childhood was anything but ordinary. One memorable day, her mother, Jackie, ended up in a wrestling match with a neighbor. Jackie, preparing for her role as Queen Anne of Austria in *The Three Musketeers*, asked Cher to let their dog, Blackie, out. Blackie bolted, only to be dragged into the neighbor's house. When Cher saw a pound truck arrive, she panicked. Jackie stormed to the truck, but the driver refused to return Blackie without a tag. Promising Cher she'd get Blackie back, Jackie confronted the neighbor. When the woman dismissed her, Jackie threatened, "I'll beat the shit out of you!" Things escalated, and soon Jackie, with her perfect ringlets, was swinging the much larger woman around the lawn by her hair. A neighbor cheered, "Go get her, blondie!" Disheveled but victorious, Jackie rescued Blackie later that night.

At nine, Cher's life unraveled further. Jackie's boyfriend, Bill, visited their home in the Valley when John, Cher's father, showed up unexpectedly. Hearing the back door slam, John thought Bill was escaping and stormed in, missing Bill entirely. Enraged, John stabbed Bill's Cadillac with a butcher knife. Jackie, barefoot, helped Cher and baby Gee climb over the backyard fence to escape. Jackie ripped off a toenail in her rush and banged on a stranger's door, begging, "Please let us in. My husband's trying to kill me!" The police arrived but let John off with a warning.

The backyard held more drama. One day, Cher landed on a sharp Yuban coffee can while flipping off a swing, slicing her leg to the bone. Blood poured as Jackie wrapped her foot in towels and rushed her to the hospital. Though calm in the waiting room, Jackie fainted watching the surgeons retrieve Cher's snapped tendons. Cher's foot healed, but she was left with a distinctive gait and vivid memories of her mother's strength.

The separation from her father left a deep scar. Despite his violent outbursts, Cher adored him. She recalled his kindness, the way he loved her and Gee, and the hole he left in her life. One day he was there, and the next he was gone.

ADVENTURES AND ANTICS

Cher's first set of wheels came in the form of a tricycle. Perched on the seat, she looked at her parents, then out at the world, and thought, *I think I've learned all I can from these people. Time to go.* She pedaled furiously around the apartment complex, not actually going anywhere, but the feeling of freedom was undeniable.

That sense of independence carried over to her wild streak. By four or five, she decided to run away for real. Perched on the curb of their Laurel Canyon home with a tiny doll-sized suitcase packed with "essentials," she announced her plans to her mom. Ever calm, her mom checked on her and said, "Okay, good idea." As dusk crept in, Cher reconsidered. "I'll wait till tomorrow," she declared. Her mother simply nodded.

A few years later, living in a deep Valley apartment she hated, Cher's adventurous spirit struck again. One day, walking home from school with her friend Anita, they stumbled upon a wide-open field. Tossing aside her lunchbox–filled with the usual uninspired Wonder Bread sandwich and Fritos–Cher climbed the fence to greet an old dappled gray horse. With Anita's help, she clambered onto its swayback. The two girls rode the sweet creature across the pasture until they reached a barbed-wire fence marking the end of the field.

But the adventure didn't stop there. Beyond the fence lay railway tracks and a row of stationary boxcars. Without hesitation, Cher boosted Anita onto one. Inside, it felt like stepping into an outlaw movie. Dirty straw littered the floor, and it smelled musty. Giggling, they settled into a corner, imagining the stories they'd tell. Then the train began to move.

As the boxcar rolled out of town, Cher was thrilled. "This is way better than horseback riding!" she exclaimed. Anita, on the other hand, began to panic. By the time the train slowed near Santa Ana, the light was fading, and Anita was in tears. They jumped down, found a railroad worker, and called their mothers.

Cher's mom's initial relief turned to anger mid-call. "Cherilyn, what did you do?" she demanded. By the time she drove the forty miles to pick them up, she was fuming. Spotting Cher, she yelled, "And what did you do with your lunchbox?" Cher shrugged and said, "I threw it away. It was just an adventure."

Later, grounded and reflecting on her day, Cher thought, *I borrowed a horse and jumped on a train . . . and it was worth it.* Her antics had become so legendary that her mom and Mamaw joked about placing bets on whether she'd make it to twenty-one.

Cher's antics were endless. Once, she mailed a potato bug to her uncle Mickey, who was terrified of insects. When he opened the envelope, he screamed, chased Cher outside, and smashed the bug in her face. Another time, when a tarantula wandered into their Laurel Canyon home, Mickey jumped onto the couch, yelling, "Get it, George! Get it!" Jackie swatted it with a broom, but the legs kept moving.

CHAPTER 4

JOURNEY OF GROWTH

BOYS, BUTTERFLIES, AND BROKEN HEARTS

Just before Cher turned ten, her family moved into a small redwood bungalow on Beeman Avenue, which quickly became her favorite home. It had the charm of a mountain cabin, with knotty pine paneling, a real fireplace, and apricot and peach trees in the yard. Her mom, determined to make it cozy, learned to wallpaper in a day and decorated the room Cher shared with Gee in powder-blue butterflies that matched their bedspreads. To Cher, it felt like they were rich.

The best part of living there was having Jake, her mom's best friend, close by. Jake, a former singer who entertained troops during the war, was like a second mother to Cher. Fun and spontaneous, Jake threw potluck parties on a whim and never lost her temper. Cher adored her, not just for her generosity in sharing movie-star magazines, but for her warm presence. Jake's son, Kevin, often played with Gee, despite their differences–Gee always had her head in a book, while Kevin caused trouble.

When Kevin burned circles into the leather seats of her mom's Cadillac with a lighter, Cher's mom was furious. But Jake, ever calm, just said, "George, come on, it's done." Her steady demeanor was a comfort to everyone around her.

Decades later, when Jake was dying, Cher rushed to her side. Shaking Jake's foot, she teased, "Hey, what the fuck do you think you're doing?" Jake smiled, and by the time Cher left, she was singing her favorite song, "All the Things You Are," one last time.

The Beeman property, owned by a kind Southern couple, became a refuge. The family moved in and out of the house three times, depending on Mom's ability to afford the rent. Cher's Uncle Mickey and his wife, Rita, sometimes lived with them. Mickey, funny and charming, danced with Rita in their tiny living room, introducing Cher to Tito Puente's music.

Fourth of July barbecues were a highlight, filled with Southern fried chicken, corn on the cob, and firecrackers. For Halloween, Cher wore her mom's peasant skirt and blouse, and for the first time, she wore lipstick and mascara. Looking in the mirror, she was amazed by her transformation.

Cher's creative spark flourished at Beeman. She put on plays in the living room with Gee as her assistant. Inspired by her mother's time in drama school, Cher dreamed of the stage, though her shy nature made her love of performing surprising.

For her tenth birthday, Mom decorated the front lawn with balloons and a lollipop tree, and Mamaw brought the traditional $1.79 bakery cake. But the highlight of the day came when Mom drove off in their old Pontiac and returned with a maroon English racing bike. Barefoot and wearing her new two-piece bathing suit, Cher jumped on the bike and rode off, leaving her party behind.

Hours later, when she returned at sunset, her mom sat waiting on the porch. "Everyone's gone, Cher. Did you have a good time?"

She did. The Beeman house was more than a home; it was where her imagination and independence truly began to bloom.

At ten years old, Cher's world was shifting. Her awareness of boys grew, and with it came a mischievous streak. Milton Broadlight, a fifth-grader, brought her a corsage for what was essentially a playdate and even kissed her at the end. "Well, that was okay," she thought. Another boy, Yan Kovaleski, gifted her a flower, perfume, and soap. "He must be rich," she concluded, dazzled by his generosity.

While boys intrigued her, home life was defined by her mother's unwavering determination. Mom's dates were fewer, but Lou stood out as a favorite for his humor and his knack for helping with school projects. Protective as ever, her mother constantly warned, "Don't talk to strangers. Never get in someone's car, even if they have candy or a puppy." Cher, however, had her quirks. She'd fret about matching silverware in drawers, fearing a big fork might bully a smaller one. Her mother, often at her wit's end, would sigh, "Cher, it's just a voice. No one can hurt you on the telephone."

For her eleventh birthday, Cher's mother gifted her a beautiful skirt and blouse set–sky blue with white clouds that morphed into flowers. Proud of her outfit, Cher wore it to Sunday school during one of her mother's "explore every religion" phases. Afterward, she and her sister, Gee, dashed to the local convenience store for free birthday treats. They forgot that their mother was picking them up from church, and when someone mistakenly told her a man had taken them, she panicked, searching the neighborhood in tears. When she finally found them at home enjoying their treats, she retreated to her room, crying loudly behind a closed door. Cher, ashamed and sorry, let her mother grieve in peace.

Life became harder when her mother could no longer afford their home. Cher and Gee moved in with their grandparents, Mamaw and Pa, in La Puente. While Pa taught Cher to drive his Ford, the rough school environment terrified her. Once, she escaped a gang of girls wielding scissors to cut others' hair. Another time, a jealous classmate pushed her head into a locker and threatened a fight in a vacant lot. As the group gathered, Cher heard a car horn. Her mother had arrived just in time, shouting, "Get in!" Cher obeyed, and they sped away.

Separated from her mother for four months, Cher felt lost. Her mother, living in a tiny garage apartment, struggled too, enduring panic attacks in her solitude. Over dinner one Sunday, Cher broke down. "I can't do this anymore, Mom. I want to live with you," she sobbed. Her mother, near tears, explained, "I have nothing–just a mattress. Child welfare would take you." Defeated but understanding, Cher returned to her grandparents' house and wept silently in the bath. That longing stayed with her for years, making every reunion with her mother all the more precious.

BAREFOOT DREAMS

School was a mixed bag for Cher–she excelled in sports like kickball and dodgeball, yet often felt isolated as the poorest kid in class. Her saddle shoes, patched with cardboard and rubber bands, were a constant reminder of her family's struggles. One day, unable to bear the humiliation, Cher begged her mom to let her stay home. Instead, her mother walked her to school, reciting, "Did you hear about the man who cried because he had no shoes until he saw the man who had no feet?" Cher's frustration with her mother's relentless perspective often made her want to scream.

Fourth grade was particularly hard after her dad left, but her history teacher, Mr. Shippo, became a beacon of kindness. His passion for history sparked her own, and he explained the Holocaust gently when she stumbled upon a haunting image in an encyclopedia. The picture of lifeless bodies piled together stuck with her forever, opening her eyes to the world's horrors. Yet, his care helped her process it.

The last day of school brought more heartache. Students traditionally dressed up, but Cher's mom couldn't afford anything new. She wore ugly brown sandals from a discount bin and an old, wrinkled pink pinafore. A cruel classmate sneered, "Oh, Cher, you decided not to dress up?" Humiliated, Cher spent the day barefoot whenever she could, vowing to one day own beautiful clothes and never feel that way again.

Her mother's thrift store finds, like a silk shirt with French cuffs, embarrassed her. Cher worried people would recognize they were secondhand. Her mom, however, dismissed her concerns, saying, "Nobody will, Cher. I've bought some of my best outfits from here." Despite their struggles, her mom's stories of her own harrowing childhood–singing on bar tops for pennies or surviving her dad's attempts to gas her–overshadowed Cher's grievances.

Even when food was scarce, her mother managed to make meals feel special with cornbread, fried chicken, and occasional treats. Cher vowed to escape poverty and take care of her family. Yet, no matter how many shoes or fancy clothes she'd own later, she would always feel happiest barefoot, carrying the resilience her mother had instilled in her.

At eleven, Cher became the unofficial head of the household when her mom was away at auditions or on set. "You're a big girl now," her mom would say. "Look after your sister." Cher had been caring for Gee since she was a baby, even surviving the time Gee ate the wheels off her toy car. While Cher's efforts weren't flawless–Gee refused to eat oranges cut the wrong way–their bond was unshakable. Gee's smile could melt Cher's heart, no matter how frustrating things got.

When their mom left for the day, always trailing perfume and hairspray, she'd remind Cher, "Never let anyone in the house." Cher would then take charge, exploring her mom's makeup and trying on oversized dresses and shoes, posing in the mirror before tackling chores. Wrapped in one of her mom's sweaters, she cleaned, washed dishes, ironed, and made the beds. Gee, meanwhile, avoided helping by asking for instructions on folding shirts or fixing pillows, leaving Cher to handle it all.

Mealtimes were simple–BLTs, grilled cheese, or peanut butter and jelly. Cher's cooking repertoire remained limited, though her homemade pasta sauce, "Diva Pasta Sauce," eventually became a gift for friends. Being left in charge gave her a sense of control amidst their struggles. While she couldn't pay rent or buy groceries, keeping the house in order became her way of contributing, a small anchor of stability in a chaotic world.

It was during this time that Cher first fell seriously ill, stricken by a virus that penicillin couldn't cure. For two feverish weeks, she endured hallucinations as her temperature climbed to 103 degrees. With her mother working on the movie *Bundle of Joy*, Mamaw stepped in, tending to Cher with cold water compresses and aspirin. The doctor remained baffled, but Mamaw's care eventually pulled her through.

Returning to school, Cher discovered she could earn free lunches by working in the cafeteria. Though embarrassed, she quietly bagged cookies or did chores, then joined her friends by the football bleachers. It comforted her to realize that being cool mattered more than being rich.

Schoolwork, however, was a constant struggle. Spelling and grammar eluded her; punctuation felt random, and books remained unread until she turned seventeen. Teachers insisted she wasn't "applying herself," but Cher knew that wasn't true. What no one realized was her undiagnosed learning disability, a condition without a name then. The phrase "apply yourself" became a lifelong trigger, fueling her frustration at the world's unfair expectations.

Math was even worse, like a foreign language she couldn't grasp. Her mother, unbothered by a D on her report card, reassured her, "Don't worry, babe. When you grow up, you'll have someone to do numbers for you." That endearing "babe" became a family trademark, inspiring the title of "I Got You, Babe."

Years later, even military time baffled her, and a boyfriend's dismissive "You're not applying yourself" led her to walk out mid-conversation. That phrase remained intolerable, a reminder of the uphill battles she had always fought–and overcome.

CHRISTMAS MIRACLES

Grandma Lynda, now married to Grandpa Charlie, was still working as a waitress while Charlie baked at Johnston's Pies. Cher adored him for his playful kindness, like the time he let her devour an entire chocolate cream pie despite Lynda's protests. Though Charlie might have helped their struggling family, Lynda never let him know. She'd only step in when they were desperate. Still, Cher managed a bond with her grandmother, even enduring the grooming of Lynda's pampered poodles, Samson and Chanson, to stay on her good side.

Whenever her mom got a tax refund, life felt magical. They'd head to a mom-and-pop store in the Valley where Cher bought art supplies, including her prized box of sixty-four Crayola crayons. She never used them, just admired their perfect points, feeling rich for the first time. The day would end with fried shrimp at Du-par's or a trip to the drive-in, where they smuggled popcorn, watermelon, and Southern fried chicken to avoid concession stand prices. Singing old country songs together in the car, they made even waiting in line fun.

One night at the drive-in, her mom introduced *The Wizard of Oz.*

Cher's initial disappointment at the black-and-white film vanished when Dorothy stepped into the vibrant world of color. The film's message of courage and magic stayed with her forever. Another night, *Psycho* left a very different impression. Days later, Gee terrified Cher in the shower by pretending to be Norman Bates, earning a spanking from their furious mom.

Christmas, no matter their financial state, was always special. In 1954, their new apartment on Bakman Avenue felt like a step backward, but her mom didn't let that dampen their holiday spirit. With help from Nudie Cohn, a kind designer famous for Elvis's gold lamé suit, her mom returned home with dolls, cowboy boots, jeans, and fringe jackets. A photograph of Cher and Gee wearing their new outfits captured their joy. It was a Christmas Cher would never forget, filled with love, resilience, and just a touch of magic.

CHAPTER 5

A SHADOW OF THE PAST

A GLIMPSE OF LUXURY

In the summer of 1957, Cher's life took a glamorous turn when her mother, Georgia, married real estate magnate Joseph Harper Collins. Joe was a larger-than-life character, barrel-chested and endlessly charming, who adored Georgia and her daughters. The whirlwind romance began at a party and led to a wedding at the quaint Little Brown Church in the Valley. Soon after, the family moved into Joe's opulent pink Beverly Hills mansion, complete with live-in housekeepers and a heated swimming pool.

For Cher, the pool was a dream come true, and the lavish lifestyle was unlike anything she'd ever known. Joe's love for entertaining meant the house was always buzzing with friends, family, and barbecues by the pool. Cher, her sister Gee, and Georgia found themselves laughing constantly, their bond so strong that others often mistook them for sisters. For a fleeting moment, their lives were carefree, filled with steak dinners, new clothes, and even lobster as a summer staple. Georgia, finally free from the stress of money and work, radiated happiness.

Yet beneath the glamour, cracks began to form. Joe's penchant for partying and his adventurous ideas about their marriage shocked Georgia, who couldn't reconcile her values with his. Despite their deep affection for each other, the marriage unraveled. "I love you, Joe," Georgia told him, "but I can't do that."

When the family packed up to leave Joe's home, Cher felt heartbroken. They had been so happy, and Joe had been a wonderful father figure. Even after the divorce, Joe's generosity shone through. He rented them a beautiful house with a cutting-edge sound system and ensured they had support. Though their time with Joe was brief, he left a lasting impression, proving to be a class act even as their paths diverged.

THE MISSING PIECE

Cher's mother's announcement came out of nowhere one evening: "How'd you like to meet your real father?" It was said so casually, yet the man in question, Johnnie Sarkisian, had been nothing more than a shadowy figure in her life. Cher was skeptical but agreed, curious to meet the man she knew almost nothing about.

The next day, her mother dressed her in her Sunday best, complete with curled hair, making Cher abandon her roller rink plans. When the doorbell rang, Cher opened it to find Johnnie standing there, dark-haired and well-dressed, with a confident smile. For the first time, she saw herself in someone else–her olive skin, almond-shaped eyes, and heart-shaped mouth mirrored back at her. His resemblance to Victor Mature, her favorite actor, made it all the more surreal.

"So, this is my baby?" he asked cheerfully. Intrigued by his alligator loafers, Cher's first words to her father were about their cost: $1,100–a sum that left her speechless. Her own prized roller skates cost a mere $21.

Johnnie stayed for dinner, and Cher watched him closely, noticing their shared traits. He ate slowly, smiled with the same half-smile, and had a calm demeanor unlike her fiery mother and sister. For Cher, seeing Johnnie felt like finding a missing puzzle piece, revealing parts of herself she couldn't explain before.

Though she liked him, the idea of calling him "Dad" didn't sit right. He was something else, something new. When her mother remarried Johnnie and let him move in, Cher struggled to adjust to the sudden changes, feeling uneasy about how fast it all happened. While Johnnie was kind and easygoing, Cher's emotions remained tangled, her love for her absent daddy complicating the newfound connection.

Cher struggled to understand her mother's enduring connection to Johnnie Sarkisian–a man who had gambled away their security, abandoned them, and only reappeared when he thought there was money to gain. "Why go back for more?" Cher wondered, imagining the absurdity of forgiving such betrayal. Yet, her mother, like many women of her generation, clung to the notion that marriage equaled safety, even if it meant repeating the same mistakes.

When Johnnie returned, Cher saw through his charm. To her, he was all smooth words and little substance. He was warm and kind, but he brought no skills, no stability–just excuses. Still, he tried to win her over, inviting her to lunch and ordering her favorite malt. Soft-spoken and calculated, he revealed a turbulent past: years in prison, heroin addiction, and the fraud that landed him there. He even lifted his shirt to show her the scar from the surgery that had started his downward spiral. Cher listened but remained skeptical. Her mother might have fallen for his remorse, but Cher refused to be so easily swayed.

As Johnnie spoke, Cher's mind wandered to the roller rink and Foxy, the boy she had a crush on, waiting to see her skate. She felt no urge to embrace this man who looked like her but was still a stranger. She resolved to keep her distance, not ready to trust someone who seemed too polished, too smooth.

Not long after, Johnnie convinced her mother to marry him again and relocate to Little Armenia in Fresno, where they would live with his family—strangers Cher had never met. Mamaw put Cher and Gee on a train alone, sending them off to a new chapter in an unfamiliar world, filled with uncertainty. For Cher, it felt like yet another upheaval orchestrated by a man who had already failed them once.

A NEW WORLD

Cher got her first period on the train to Fresno, and with no idea how to use a tampon, she stuffed toilet paper into her underpants. As she walked through the club car, the train's overhead lights exposed her worst nightmare—all the paper fell out under her skirt. Mortified, she whispered to Gee to pick them up, who giggled as she delicately retrieved them one by one. Cher couldn't believe she survived the embarrassment by the time they arrived.

In Fresno, Cher met her Armenian family for the first time. She was astonished at how much they looked like her. Dozens of relatives gathered at her grandparents' home, doting on her and stroking her hair, speaking mostly Armenian but radiating warmth. For the first time, it was her mother and Gee who felt like outsiders.

Johnnie's return to his family was strategic; bringing Cher was his redemption move. As the prodigal son, he regained favor, despite having gambled away the family business. Cher recognized his charm but knew she was part of his calculated comeback.

Still, she relished the experience. She bonded with her grandparents and learned to make Armenian delicacies like sarma and lahmajoun. Watching her father and his sisters cook nightly banquets amazed her. For once, Cher felt like she belonged, embraced by a family that was entirely hers.

For a time, life in Fresno felt normal. Cher lived in her own house, attended a school she didn't hate, and played with new friends near an aqueduct. They snuck into orchards for fruit, cooling peaches and plums in the water before eating them. Though she missed her Beeman friends, this brief period of stability made Fresno almost enjoyable. But soon, they moved again—this time to Las Vegas, where they lived with Aunt Roxy, Uncle Vincent, and cousins Dickie and Geralyn.

Aunt Roxy was larger than life, fearless and funny, with a booming laugh. Cher admired her instantly. The family's dry-cleaning business inside the Tropicana, Las Vegas's grandest hotel, gave Cher a taste of the city's glamor. Life there, with its bustling family and endless buffets, began to feel like a new home. But Johnnie ruined it all, as he always did.

Unbeknownst to anyone, he'd fallen back into gambling and heroin, eventually pawning off Mom's precious jewelry for drugs. The breaking point came when Johnnie, high and careless, set his bed on fire while preparing a fix. Smoke filled the house, and Mom grabbed Cher and Gee in a panic, screaming not about the fire but at Johnnie, who was too stoned to respond. That night, they fled Vegas and returned to Beeman.

Cher never questioned the abrupt departure or asked about seeing her Armenian family again. She knew Johnnie was trouble–a man her mother always hoped would change but never did. Back in Beeman, Mom discovered she was pregnant by Johnnie, leading to another illegal abortion that nearly killed her.

Cher, too young to understand, sensed the danger as she glimpsed Mom confined to her darkened room, girlfriends whispering in and out. Fear gripped Cher, but against all odds, her mother recovered–only to let Johnnie back into their lives once more.

TEENAGE REBELLION

During a break from Johnnie, Cher's mom moved them into a grand Georgian-style house in Toluca Lake near Bob's Big Boy. The home, with its high ceilings, brick chimney, and a massive Christmas tree on the lawn, felt like a dream. They shared the space with her mom's friend Colleen and her daughter Paulette. Cher admired Colleen's zen demeanor and bohemian style, even mirroring her morning ritual of sipping Constant Comment tea in peaceful silence–until her mom inevitably disrupted it with chatter.

At thirteen, Cher's rebellious streak emerged when she skipped school to joyride in her mom's red Pontiac convertible. With Gee as her passenger, she navigated Hollywood Boulevard, ran red lights, and dented trash cans but returned home unscathed. Her confidence grew until she was caught sneaking home by her mom, who, miraculously, didn't notice her car had been taken. "Oh, hi, girls," her mom said casually. Cher realized she'd gotten away with it, thanking her lucky stars.

Soon after, Johnnie's influence led Cher to Villa Cabrini, a strict Catholic boarding school. While Cher initially loved the uniforms, which shielded her from being judged, the restrictions on makeup and clothes frustrated her. Nicknamed “Pinky Sarkisian” for her sole pink pinafore, Cher’s humor often got her into trouble, especially when jokes about nuns reached the mother superior. Punished to walk on her knees reciting the rosary, Cher’s comedy career at school ended.

Cher enjoyed the camaraderie and mischief with friends like Anita and Rose, but when she told her mom about being slapped by the mother superior, her mom’s memories of past abuse resurfaced. Determined to protect her daughter, she pulled Cher from Villa Cabrini, despite Cher’s protests. Against Johnnie’s wishes, Cher was sent back to public school, leaving behind newfound friendships and a taste of belonging.

In January 1959, Cher started at Walter Reed school, one of the many schools her sister Gee kept track of, claiming she’d attended over twenty-five. Life as a teenager in the Valley was a mix of adventure and lessons learned the hard way. One night, Cher and her friends borrowed a boyfriend’s ’57 Chevy outside a bowling alley. When he didn’t return, they drove off, stopping at Johnie’s drive-in for orange juice to mix with vodka. A police car appeared behind them, its lights flashing, and Cher found herself hauled to the station after the boyfriend reported the car stolen.

While her friends’ parents arrived quickly, Cher’s mother couldn’t be reached. Hours later, an officer moved her to a holding room with a bunk, only for a hand to grab her ankle from underneath. A drunk man had been forgotten in the room. After screaming for help, Cher was rescued, and her mom arrived at 2 a.m. Despite the ordeal, her mother saw her tear-stained face and decided she’d been punished enough. Yet, the incident cost Cher her friends, whose parents deemed her a bad influence. Years later, a photo of her from junior high was doctored to resemble a mugshot, spreading as an early case of “fake news.”

Despite her confident exterior, Cher wasn’t as worldly as she seemed. As she matured, unwanted attention from older men became frighteningly common. Colleen’s boyfriend Huntz, an actor nearly forty, made an advance during a car ride. Cher pushed him away, threatening to tell her mom. Though he brushed it off, Cher doubted herself and apologized. Another instance involved Gabe, her mother’s boyfriend, who took her for a joyful motorcycle ride, treating her to sundaes at Wil Wright’s. Later, he confessed to Georgia that he was in love with Cher. Heartbroken, Georgia threw him out but, in her pain, accused Cher of leading him on and kicked her out of the house. Cher stayed with a friend until her mother calmed down, but the incident left her feeling hurt and betrayed.

Though Cher craved to feel attractive, she never imagined being seen that way by men much older. She longed to be attractive but struggled with unwanted attention from men who should've known better.

FIRST CRUSHES

When Fred Smith, the school's cutest football star, asked Cher out, she was thrilled. Dressed in a mocha shirtdress her mom bought for the occasion, she felt fabulous as Fred drove her to a party. They shared a kiss, but the date ended disastrously when Fred drank too much beer and threw up on her front lawn. Yet Cher held his head, still happy he'd chosen her. Embarrassed, Fred never spoke to her again.

Fortunately, Cher had other distractions. She had a crush on a neighborhood boy who worked on his hot rod. They kissed often, but when he dismissed her in front of his friends, she decided to "loan out" her virginity to him out of spite. The experience, underwhelming and transactional, left her unimpressed. "Is that it?" she asked before sending him away for good.

Cher's misadventures didn't end there. After moving into a new duplex near Pink's, she met Richard, a charming actor who introduced her to malt liquor. Unaware of its potency, she drank too much and threw up all over the stage at a theater. Richard cared for her, but his friend's attempt to kiss her mid-illness left her both horrified and amused.

Amid these chaotic moments, Cher discovered her love for *West Side Story*. When her mom brought back the soundtrack from New York, Cher played it endlessly, creating dances and imagining herself as part of the musical's story. The passion and romance of Tony and Maria became her ideal, far removed from the awkward advances of teenage boys.

Life changed abruptly again when her mom announced plans to marry Gilbert LaPiere, a banker from New York. With the decision made, Cher and Gee were uprooted once more, leaving Los Angeles behind. Though Cher dreaded losing her independence, she was excited to move to the city she had only seen in movies–her very own West Side Story.

CHAPTER 6

FROM DREAMS TO INDEPENDENCE

MANHATTAN MAGIC AND HARD LESSONS

Manhattan was a new chapter for Cher and her family. The flight alone was unforgettable, with Cher and Gee marveling at the luxury of first-class–multi-course meals, crisp stewardess uniforms, and a thrilling view from the window seat. But while the girls delighted in their first airplane ride, their mother had a full-blown panic attack mid-flight, gripping Gilbert's arm so tightly that a doctor had to administer oxygen.

Once they landed, her mom's mood lifted as they settled into a sleek apartment on East 56th Street, above a D'Agostino supermarket. Cher and Gee each had their own bedrooms, and the views from their high-rise windows made the city feel alive. Cher was enchanted by Manhattan's energy. Unlike LA, New York offered freedom: no car needed, just the thrill of walking the bustling streets or hailing a cab. Her mom, adjusting to Gilbert's sophisticated lifestyle, found joy in the city's glamour–plays, fine dining, and entertaining friends in their stylish apartment.

Cher spent her first New York Christmas spinning 45s on her new record player. When elevator operator Jesse invited her to a New Year's Eve party, her mother surprisingly agreed. A mishap while bleaching her mom's hair left Cher with blond streaks, but her mom evened it out, leaving her with a new look that delighted her. Dressed in her mother's mink coat, she set off for her first Manhattan party, feeling grown-up and confident.

The East Village party was like stepping into *West Side Story*. The boys in sharp suits and the girls with sky-high hair and tight dresses captivated Cher. Jesse was a gentleman, but the party took a dramatic turn when a man, stabbed during a kitchen fight, stumbled into the living room. Though shocking, it felt thrilling, like watching the Sharks and Jets come to life.

A few nights later, Cher went on a date with one of Jesse's friends, a Bernardo lookalike. The date soured quickly when he took her to his bleak apartment and tried to force himself on her. Cher managed to push him away, firmly saying, "Stop. I'm not doing this." She escaped unharmed but shaken, vowing never to put herself in such a dangerous situation again–though deep down, she knew she might.

Life in New York brought change, excitement, and some friction for Cher. When Gilbert adopted Cher and Gee, her mother was thrilled, but Cher struggled with being "Cher LaPiere"—a name she thought sounded silly—and resented Gilbert's strict, traditional rules. After years of being treated like an adult by her mother, the sudden shift to childlike restrictions felt patronizing. Smoking, previously allowed, was suddenly banned, and Cher felt the sting of her mother's feigned ignorance.

Starting at a new high school was another challenge. On her first snowy day, she arrived by cab—a faux pas that almost got her beaten up for being a "pussy." Feeling alienated and out of place, she quit after three weeks, convincing her parents that school wasn't working. Though relieved, Cher now had no outlet for meeting new people until Gilbert introduced her to Joyce, a colleague's daughter. Joyce's sophisticated circle of Upper West Side friends welcomed Cher, giving her a taste of New York's glamorous social life—dancing at nightclubs, shopping sprees, and carefree outings.

For Cher's fifteenth birthday, Gilbert took the family to see Eartha Kitt at the Persian Room in the Plaza Hotel. Watching Eartha's magnetic performance in a sequined dress, commanding the audience's attention, was transformative. It gave Cher a glimpse of what she wanted for herself: power, poise, and the ability to mesmerize.

In June, the family vacationed in Vermont, where Cher's room, conveniently far from her parents', became her own retreat. A surprise arrived in the form of Bodo, a handsome Austrian ski instructor who delivered her room service while she lounged in a camisole and panties. Embarrassed yet intrigued, Cher crossed paths with him again at dinner, where he was the maître d'. Their whirlwind romance involved Thunderbird rides and trysts, but by the time she returned to New York, she'd already lost interest.

Back in Manhattan, Cher's social calendar filled with Gilbert's cocktail parties and Broadway outings. Among the party guests was Noah Dietrich, Howard Hughes's former right-hand man, whose tales of Hughes's eccentricities fascinated everyone but left Cher only vaguely aware of Hughes's genius.

These soirées required a more polished wardrobe, prompting Gilbert to take Cher shopping. He let her choose what she loved, offering opinions and encouragement without questioning prices or styles. One standout outfit was a black-and-white polka-dot dress paired with a matching vest, a far cry from her usual jeans and crop tops. Shopping with Gilbert became a skillful dance—she let him think her choices were his ideas, ensuring a harmonious experience.

Cher embraced her evolving style, shedding casual wear for more sophisticated looks. Yet her mother's overbearing attempts to dictate her wardrobe occasionally led to frustration, as when Gilbert bought her high heels and her mother objected. Despite such moments, Cher reveled in the freedom and independence New York offered, shaping her into the poised young woman she was becoming.

FIRST LOVE AND HEARTBREAK

At fifteen, Cher became the subject of an artist's admiration when her mother commissioned Tony Mafia to sketch sepia-toned portraits of their family. Tony lavished praise on Cher's dark hair and eyes, calling them striking compared to her blonde mother and sister. Her mother's reaction to the portrait was equally flattering, even suggesting Cher should model. For the first time, Cher began to see herself as something special.

One day, while getting portfolio shots taken, she had an amusing encounter with Telly Savalas, who jokingly asked, "What would you do if I kissed you right now?" Cher rolled her eyes, and his laughter signaled his retreat.

Months later, Tony invited her to sit for a mural he was painting for Martoni's restaurant, a Hollywood hotspot. The mural depicted Italian women, and various versions of Cher graced its walls for years, though only one truly resembled her. While sitting for Tony at Martoni's, Cher caught the attention of another man—singer and musician Nino Tempo. Despite being thirteen years older, Nino's charm won her over, and their connection began to blossom.

Their budding romance was interrupted when Nino's friend, Phillip Spector, arrived from New York. Phillip, an emerging music producer, demanded Nino's constant presence at Gold Star Recording Studios. Cher grew suspicious of Nino's excuses, convinced he was seeing someone else. She didn't yet understand Phillip's revolutionary work in music, creating the iconic "Wall of Sound."

To prove his honesty, Nino took Cher to meet Phillip at his Sunset Boulevard hotel. Phillip's behavior left Cher unimpressed, particularly when he smirked and asked, "Voulez-vous coucher avec moi?" Cher's sharp response, "Oui, pour l'argent," stunned him into silence.

Their relationship ended soon after, with Nino lamenting, "You broke my heart, Cher." Though he was a good man, Cher couldn't believe he was merely a "babysitter" to another. Later, she was genuinely happy for Nino when he and his sister won a Grammy for *Deep Purple.*

BACK TO LA

Gilbert often acted as a mediator between Cher and her mother, especially as her mother's homesickness for Los Angeles began to strain their lives in New York. Cher enjoyed her newfound freedom in Manhattan, but her mother's misery made life at home unbearable. The tension finally erupted during a dinner table disagreement. Cher corrected her mother on a small detail of a story, which led to an uncharacteristic outburst. In a moment of frustration, her mother slapped her across the mouth. Unfortunately, the ruby and pearl ring Gilbert had bought her cut Cher's lip.

Shocked and hurt, Cher stormed out of the apartment, her bleeding lip a painful reminder of how much her mother was struggling. Even Gilbert seemed stunned, and it was clear to everyone that the situation was unsustainable. Cher knew her mother needed to return to LA, and soon after, her mother declared that she couldn't handle another East Coast winter. She felt trapped in their high-rise and longed for the sun and familiarity of California.

Gilbert, always accommodating, agreed to move back, transferring to the LA branch of his bank. When the family arrived, Cher's mother kissed the ground in joy–a moment so dramatic that it was captured in a photograph. Gilbert bought a Cadillac and a sprawling house on Estrondo Drive in Encino, complete with a pool, gardens, and a view of Clark Gable's estate.

Back in LA, Cher's mother thrived, reconnecting with old friends and immersing herself in the glamorous social life she had missed. For Cher, the return was bittersweet. While she was happy to see her mother happy again, she mourned the loss of the independence she had enjoyed in New York. LA's reliance on cars made her New York freedom seem like a distant memory, a part of her life she wasn't ready to leave behind.

Cher's life was changing dramatically. Living in Los Angeles without a car was stifling, but after passing her driving test in Gilbert's Buick Skylark, she embraced newfound freedom. Driving gave her independence, and Cher seized it, leaving school behind after a suspension for refusing to remove her sunglasses–an homage to her idol Holly Golightly. Her principal saw potential in her, saying, "There's something good in you," but Cher knew traditional school wasn't her path.

One night on Sunset Boulevard, Cher's driving adventure took an unexpected turn when a white Lincoln convertible cut her off. Furious, she confronted the driver–none other than Warren Beatty, the heartthrob actor of *Splendor in the Grass*. Despite being grounded for staying out late after their impromptu date, Cher melted her mother's anger when Warren personally called to smooth things over. Though they only went on a few dates, his charm left a lasting impression.

Her parents insisted she return to school, enrolling her at Montclair College Prep in Tarzana. Much to Cher's disappointment, her mother and Gilbert insisted she finish school, enrolling her at Montclair College Prep in Tarzana. The only highlights were her French lessons with Mrs. Simpson, who admired her natural ear for languages, and drama and singing with Mr. di Fiori. When the school announced a performance of *The Mikado*, Cher eagerly auditioned for the lead role of Yum-Yum. However, she was crushed when Mr. di Fiori placed her in the chorus instead. "You're a contralto, Cher," he explained, citing her unique vocal range. Disheartened, Cher thought, *Well, that's the end of that dream.*

To channel her energy, Cher's mom enrolled her in Jeff Corey's renowned acting workshop. Initially skeptical, Jeff dismissed her for being too young, but Cher's determination won him over. Assigned *Of Mice and Men*, she struggled but persevered, eventually earning a spot in his class–the youngest he'd ever accepted.

Jeff was notoriously tough on Cher, frequently pushing her limits. When she confronted him, he embraced her and said, "Because you're the best in the class, Cher. You're an actor, and I'm so proud of you." That moment lit a spark in her. Improv unlocked her natural talent, and Cher began to believe in herself. Jeff's advice–"Listen to what's said before you speak"–shaped her craft. For the first time, Cher realized she was more than a rebellious teenager; she had the potential to captivate and inspire.

But Cher's acting classes didn't change the tense atmosphere at home, where her mom's unhappiness loomed over everything. Trying to confide in her mother about her own struggles was often met with dismissals or comparisons to the horrors her mom had endured. "At least your father didn't try to gas you!" she'd say, referencing memories of her abusive stepfather. Cher and her sister, Gee, felt powerless to help or even share their own pain, which eventually led Cher to withdraw entirely, confiding only in Gee, who offered unconditional love and understanding.

Even her mother's marriage to Gilbert, though initially happy after their return to Los Angeles, started to show cracks. Gilbert adored her mother, but Cher suspected the feeling wasn't mutual. Her mother, once vibrant and glamorous, began adopting the more conventional suburban lifestyle of her Encino neighbors–conservative clothes, therapy sessions, and a predictable routine that didn't suit her free spirit. It became clear to Cher that her mother was playing a role she didn't love.

On Cher's birthday, Gilbert gave her a $100 bill, her first ever. That week, desperate for independence, she convinced Gilbert to rent her an apartment in Beverly Hills, where she moved in with Josita, their well-meaning but hopelessly inept German maid. The Spanish-style apartment became a haven for Cher and Josita, filled with cigarette smoke, laughter, and makeshift décor made from cheap fabric. The freedom felt exhilarating, even if it came with responsibilities.

Gilbert insisted they both get jobs to contribute to rent, and Cher briefly worked as a clerk at Robinson's department store. The math-heavy job was a disaster, and after one frustrating day, she quit on the spot. Her next job, at See's Candies, brought more joy. Cher loved working in the back room, wrapping candy and assembling extravagant gift baskets while singing to herself. Still, the long hours and relentless pace wore her out, and when she fell ill with hepatitis, she had to leave the job she had grown to enjoy.

As her illness worsened, Josita left to travel with her boyfriend, leaving Cher alone and unable to afford the apartment. A jazz promoter named Red, who'd befriended her, offered her a place to stay in Laurel Canyon. Red cared for Cher during her recovery, but as she began to heal, the uncertainty of her future loomed large.

Homelessness and hopelessness weighed on Cher. Acting seemed unlikely, and her unusual singing voice didn't fit in anywhere. At sixteen, she felt lost, doubting her potential and unsure of her next move. "What the hell is to become of you, Cher?" she wondered, as life continued to batter her like a rudderless ship adrift in rough waters.

CHAPTER 7

FROM COFFEE SHOPS TO TWIN BEDS

A CHANCE MEETING AT ALDO'S

It was a weekday night in November 1962 at Aldo's coffee shop, a favorite hangout for radio promotion guys fresh from meetings with DJs upstairs at KFWB. Cher was seated with Red and her friend Melissa when a commotion erupted. Someone called out, "Hey, Sonny!" and soon everyone in the room was vying for the attention of a man yet to appear.

Expecting someone tall and dashing, Cher turned to see a charismatic figure with a Caesar-style haircut striding toward their booth. Dressed in a sharp black mohair suit, a mustard shirt with a starched collar, and matching Cuban boots, Sonny Bono was magnetic. The room seemed to fade, much like Maria and Tony's first meeting in *West Side Story*.

As Sonny sat down, Cher was struck by his charm and confidence. His long, tapered fingers adorned with a gold chain-link ID bracelet caught her attention, and his grin seemed to light up the room. She wasn't immediately in love but knew this man was special.

Everyone adored Sonny, but his focus that night was on Melissa, the stunning brunette Cher had brought along. Though he made an effort to charm her, Sonny didn't realize Melissa wasn't interested–she was gay. Still, his easy manner and quick wit captivated everyone.

Cher observed quietly, intrigued by Sonny's stories. He was the youngest of three in a Sicilian family, claimed to be descended from Napoleon Bonaparte, and had been kicked out of high school for hiring a Black band for prom. He'd held odd jobs before finding his footing in music, penning songs for artists like Sam Cooke and the Righteous Brothers.

Later, the group moved to the Red Velvet Club, where Cher lost herself on the dance floor. Sonny joined her, unable to resist her energy. "I love your clothes," she told him, admiring his black-on-black look. He complimented her T-shirt and 501 jeans, though he admitted years later that he couldn't quite figure her out that night.

Melissa's apartment, where Cher sometimes stayed, was another world–filled with stunning women, from strippers to showgirls. To Cher, Sonny seemed like he belonged in this glamorous, eclectic crowd. Though he was focused on Melissa that night, something about Sonny stayed with Cher. It wasn't love at first sight, but it was a moment she'd never forget—the first chapter of something much bigger.

A QUIRKY FRIENDSHIP AND AN UNEXPECTED REVELATION

Not long after Melissa asked Cher to move out, she spotted Sonny Bono moving into the building next door. They had only met once, but Cher was thrilled to see a familiar face. When Sonny waved her over, she ran outside, laughing at the coincidence. Over the next ten days, they became friends. Sonny appreciated her quirky, nonjudgmental nature, and Cher admired his humor and easygoing demeanor. He wasn't too grown-up despite being eleven years older and in the middle of a divorce.

When Melissa finally gave Cher her eviction deadline, Cher confided in Sonny, tears welling up at the thought of moving back home. Sonny, feeling sorry for her, offered her a place to stay. "If you cook and clean, you can move in with me," he said, quickly adding, "I've got twin beds, and honestly, I don't find you particularly attractive." Cher was both insulted and relieved but accepted the offer.

Living with Sonny was an education. Cher became his housekeeper and assistant, keeping out of the way when his many girlfriends visited. Sonny's relationships were casual—most women were looking for financial stability, which Sonny couldn't offer. He lived in a modest apartment, drove an old car, and shared his space with a teenager.

One of Sonny's friends eventually questioned Cher's age. When confronted, Cher lied, claiming to be seventeen and almost eighteen. Sonny accepted her explanation, though her guilty expression likely gave her away. Their friendship continued, with Sonny taking care of her when she was sick and ensuring she felt safe.

Despite Sonny's teasing about her thin frame, Cher grew attached to him, feeling that he was someone who would always look out for her. Their bond became familial, with Cher seeing Sonny as a mix of brother and father. One night, after a panic attack triggered by the silence of a blank TV screen, Cher confessed her fear. Sonny groggily invited her into his bed, warning her, "Just sleep, okay?" That night, as she lay beside him, she felt safe—a dynamic that would define their relationship for years to come.

Sonny became a guiding force in Cher's life, encouraging her to conquer her long-held resistance to reading. He introduced her to *The Saracen Blade* by Frank Yerby, a story set in Sicily during a time of peaceful coexistence among three religions. With Sonny's advice to read at her own pace, Cher discovered the joy of reading for pleasure. Completing her first book was a revelation, and it ignited a lifelong appreciation for stories. She began to admire Sonny deeply, even hero-worshipping him, though the feeling wasn't mutual.

Sonny enjoyed Cher's offbeat humor and embraced activities she loved, such as painting, sculpting with clay, or having picnics in the park—interests his girlfriends had little patience for. Cher also bonded with Sonny's young daughter, Christy, and his beloved Yorkshire terrier, Scunci, whenever they visited. Sonny was a doting father, and his love for Christy showed Cher a softer side of him.

However, Sonny's reluctance to go dancing puzzled Cher. He once loved dancing but grew uncomfortable when he realized she was better at it. While this made him possessive, Cher initially found his protectiveness thrilling, mistaking it for care. Their outings shifted to evenings at Martoni's or her Uncle Mickey's club, the Purple Onion, where Sonny mingled with industry friends. Mickey and Sonny hit it off, and Mickey kept Cher's living arrangement a secret from her mother, knowing it would cause trouble.

At home, Cher's days were filled with cleaning, singing, and listening to music. Her soundtrack included Elvis, Ray Charles, and Etta James. One day, Sonny walked in and overheard her singing. Stunned, he asked, "Was that you?" When Cher confirmed, Sonny exclaimed, "You can really sing!" Though Cher brushed off his excitement, Sonny's discovery of her voice was a turning point in their dynamic—one that would shape both their lives in the years to come.

A SHABBY STUDIO AND A MOTHER'S SUSPICION

Sonny was hustling harder than ever, working for Specialty Records while writing songs and seeking his big break. One afternoon, Cher heard honking outside and ran to the window, stunned to see Sonny behind the wheel of a bronze Cadillac convertible. "Cher! Come on! Jump in!" he yelled, his grin as wide as the car.

"What's going on? Whose car is this?" she laughed, running barefoot to meet him.

"It's ours! I got a new job!" Sonny exclaimed, delighting in her excitement as she climbed into the leather seat.

The new job was with California Record Distributors, where Sonny was soon assigned as the "artist relations representative" to the demanding Phil Spector at Gold Star Studios. Though it meant Sonny would be on call constantly, Cher couldn't help but admire his enthusiasm. He immersed himself in the world of hit-making, rubbing elbows with the legendary Wrecking Crew musicians, and often coming home with stories of cramped studios and groundbreaking tracks.

When Sonny first brought Cher to the studio, she was awestruck. "Is this really it?" she whispered, taking in the dingy room with overflowing ashtrays and cluttered instruments. Despite the mess, the energy was electric. Watching Carol Kaye on bass, Hal Blaine on drums, and Leon Russell on piano, Cher marveled at their talent. "How do they fit so many people in here?" she whispered to Sonny, standing shyly in a corner. He just smiled, snapping a photo of her against the wall.

Sonny's role wasn't glamorous–playing tambourines, rattling a mule's jawbone, and fetching coffee–but he saw it as an invaluable education. "You couldn't pay for this kind of experience," he told her, shrugging off the lackey treatment with his usual humor.

One day, Cher's carefully managed independence faced a challenge when her mother made a surprise visit. Unaware of Cher's living situation with Sonny, her mom arrived unannounced, eager to meet the "airline stewardess" Cher had described as her roommate. Panic set in as Cher realized she couldn't hide the truth forever.

Between the pressures of Sonny's relentless schedule and her mother's growing suspicions, Cher's world was on the brink of an unexpected confrontation, one that threatened to upend the carefully balanced life she'd built.

Cher's delicate balancing act of hiding her living arrangement with Sonny from her mother came to an abrupt end one day when her mom showed up unannounced. Cher scrambled, frantically tossing Sonny's clothes out the window to Melissa's apartment and stuffing his underwear in the tea cupboard. Letting her mom in, Cher barely had time to compose herself before she heard, "I think I'll make a cup of tea."

Panic-stricken, Cher dashed to the cupboard. "No, Mom! You're in my place now. Let me make the tea!" Her mother's suspicion deepened. Pushing Cher aside, she opened the cupboard and pulled out Sonny's underwear. Her glare said it all.

"Well, his name is Sonny," Cher stammered. "He's separated, and he's just letting me crash here. Nothing's going on!"

Her mother stormed into the bedroom, spotting the twin beds. "Bullshit!" she declared. "You're coming home with me." Cher had no choice but to leave, curling up in despair back in her old bedroom.

Desperate to keep Cher from seeing Sonny, her mother consulted a therapist, who advised against forbidding the relationship outright. Instead, she whisked Cher and Gee off to Arkansas for a visit with family. But Cher's experience there only fueled her frustrations, especially when a family friend deliberately kicked dust at a group of Black girls. Cher protested, but her mom cautioned, "You're not going to change their minds, babe."

Back in LA, Cher called Sonny, devastated to learn his beloved Yorkie, Scunci, had passed away. "I miss you," he admitted, and her heart soared. But her joy was short-lived. When Sonny brought her home past curfew, her mother stood waiting. "You do know she's only seventeen?" she yelled. "I'll call the police and have you thrown in jail!" The revelation of Cher's true age left Sonny exasperated. "Sheesh, Cher!" he groaned.

Fearing the police, Sonny kept his distance, and Cher's mother sent her to the Hollywood Studio Club, a strict, chaperoned residence for aspiring actresses. Though her new home boasted a storied history, Cher felt miserable, sneaking out to meet Sonny whenever she could. Despite their separation, their bond remained unshaken. Sonny missed their connection as much as she did, leaving Cher longing for the man she realized meant more to her than anyone else.

WHEN THE LINES WERE CROSSED

Cher's life took another sharp turn when her mother discovered that Gilbert had left her for Beverly, one of her closest friends. The betrayal shattered her. Inconsolable and furious, she spiraled into depression, unable to cope with yet another failed marriage and the looming reality of having to work again as her fortieth birthday approached.

At just seventeen, Cher stepped up once more to shoulder the burden. Her younger sister, Gee, finally emerged from her "horse haze" and recognized the gravity of their situation, but Cher remained the stabilizing force. Memories of comforting her mother during past struggles resurfaced, from nights of worry over money to the time she nearly died after an abortion. It was exhausting and heartbreaking.

A letter from Gilbert announcing he'd moved to Oklahoma City with Beverly and planned to sell the house was enough to shake her mother out of despair. She whisked Cher and Gee on a manic shopping spree, maxing out her credit cards. While Cher treasured the velvet jacket and turquoise blouse she picked, her mother's eventual theft of them left her hurt and angry.

Returning to the Studio Club to gather her things, Cher was reunited with Sonny, who took her to see *The Balcony.* Watching her acting teacher, Jeff Corey, make his comeback after being blacklisted filled her with joy. But what caught her off guard was Sonny's kiss afterward. It was a moment that changed everything, marking a shift in their relationship that neither could ignore.

CHAPTER 8

THE EARLY JOURNEY OF SONNY AND CHER

STEPPING BACK AND FINDING HER VOICE

Phillip Spector, known for his mercurial moods, commanded respect in the studio. His quirks were legendary, and while he could erupt in frustration, he could also dissolve into laughter, as he did when a tape was ruined by spilled coffee. The studio thrived on maintaining a light atmosphere, where Phillip's focus always remained on the music. Cher, immersed in this dynamic, learned to navigate his personality, exchanging deadpan retorts with him until Sonny urged her to hold back. Yet, Phillip appreciated her spirit, eventually letting her hang out in the booth—a sign of his growing respect.

Life at home felt increasingly strained for Cher. Her mother's silent disapproval contrasted sharply with the respect she found among the musicians at Gold Star. When Sonny introduced her to the studio, she was awestruck by the tight, smoky space filled with legendary musicians like the Wrecking Crew. Cher was nervous but captivated by their energy and talent.

In the summer of 1963, when Darlene Love missed a session, Phillip, desperate to keep the schedule, told Sonny and Cher to join the backup singers. Nervously stepping up to the mic, Cher froze but managed to follow the group's lead. However, Phillip soon ordered her to step back—her distinctive voice kept cutting through. This pattern repeated until she was nearly against the wall. When Darlene returned, her laughter broke the tension, but Cher's presence remained. Phillip began calling her back regularly for backup sessions, labeling her voice part of his "funk" element.

Though she sang on records for Darlene Love, the Crystals, and others, Cher often doubted herself. Take after take left her in tears, fearing she was the problem. Ronnie, Phillip's girlfriend, encouraged her, reminding Cher of her unique talent. Despite her nerves, Cher's voice became integral to the sound Phillip was crafting. Singing backup for some of the era's greatest hits, she was discovering her place in the music world.

THE BEGINNING OF SOMETHING BEAUTIFUL

Cher loved working at Gold Star, but the strain with her mother grew unbearable. Her mom, skeptical of her unpaid studio work, often accused her of lying. "If you're working, why aren't you getting paid?" she'd ask. Cher turned to Sonny, who dismissed her complaints. "You should be paying Phillip for the education you're getting!" he said. Sonny's influence became all-encompassing, discouraging Cher from acting classes and even her beloved softball games with her mom's friends.

By the summer of 1963, Sonny was her world, and his persuasion led her to sever connections with her mother's circle. Her mother, furious that her investment in acting classes was wasted, laid down a rule: no more Gold Star unless Cher was paid. The following day, Phillip noticed Cher's absence during a Christmas album session and exploded. Sonny explained the situation, and Phillip grudgingly agreed to pay Cher $25. Handing the check to her mother in triumph, Cher hoped for validation but instead saw only her mother's growing sadness.

That year, her mother's depression deepened after Gilbert's departure, and Cher finally reached her breaking point. Packing her belongings, she left home, escaping through her bedroom window to Sonny's apartment. "What's your mom gonna do about this?" Sonny asked. "Nothing," Cher replied, determined to start anew.

Living with Sonny, Cher adjusted to her new life. She borrowed Sonny's until he bought her her first real outfit–a black leather jacket, a mock-turtleneck, and stirrup pants. This unconventional partnership filled a void for the both of them. High school dropouts from tumultuous homes, they shared dreams and a love for laughter.

Growing confident, Cher planned a surprise for her mother's birthday at the Purple Onion, her uncle Mickey's club. Mickey encouraged her to sing with the house band, Pat & Lolly Vegas. During rehearsals, the band was so impressed they offered her a job. Though flattered, she declined, committed to her current path. On the big night, Cher stepped on stage wearing a champagne beaded top her mom had gifted her. Singing "Danny Boy," her mother's favorite, Cher delivered a heartfelt performance.

Afterward, her mother glowed with pride. "You have a shining quality," she said. Sonny, too, was proud, seeing something special in Cher that would shape their lives together. This moment was the beginning of Cher's journey to finding her voice–on stage and in life.

In 1964, Cher and Sonny worked closely with Phillip Spector, witnessing the rise of the Ronettes and their tour with the Rolling Stones. Phillip returned from London sporting flashy Carnaby Street fashion that inspired Cher to embrace the glamorous Cleopatra-style look she later became famous for. Sonny, ever the strategist, decided to rebrand them as "Caesar and Cleo" to ride on the wave of Cleopatra's success.

Sonny's determination to launch Cher's career was unwavering, even as Phillip dismissed her voice as too unconventional. Sonny wrote "The Letter," which they recorded under the Caesar and Cleo moniker, but it flopped. Their next effort, a cover of "Love Is Strange," also failed to chart. Undaunted, Sonny booked them on small-time circuits, from roller rinks to bowling alleys. Cher, paralyzed with stage fright, resisted performing. "I can't," she whispered, hyperventilating. Sonny gently pushed her onstage, reassuring, "You'll be fine, Cher. You'll see." Clinging to his side, she sang through the chaos, her fear barely masked.

Beatlemania soon swept America, leaving little room for new acts. Phillip tried capitalizing on the craze by writing "Ringo, I Love You," sung by Cher under the alias Bonnie Jo Mason. The single flopped, misinterpreted as a love song between two men due to Cher's deep voice. Humiliated by her failure, Cher stopped singing at home, and Sonny ceased pushing Phillip to give her another chance.

Feeling defeated, Cher feared her career was over before it had begun, but Sonny's faith in their potential never wavered.

THE FRAGILE BONDS OF SONNY AND CHER

Cher and Sonny had settled into their new life together after moving to a small A-frame house in the hills. With its leaky shower and dark backyard, the house was far from perfect, but Cher loved making it their own. Together, they scrubbed an old brass bed frame until it gleamed and painted a table blue, transforming the space into a home. Despite their efforts, tensions simmered beneath the surface.

One evening, Sonny brought home a German shepherd puppy, but their busy schedules left little time to care for it. The dog, desperate for attention, yelped when Sonny shoved it aside. "Hey, Son, don't do that!" Cher exclaimed. Sonny spun around, pinning her against the wall. Though he didn't strike her, Cher felt her boundary had been crossed. "If you ever touch me like this again, I'll leave, and you'll never see me again," she warned. Sonny, realizing her seriousness, backed off.

Despite moments of conflict, they shared tender connections. Sonny's creative efforts–like weaving bamboo blinds into wall art–brought joy, while Cher's playful spirit lit up their home. But Sonny's growing control over Cher's life created friction. He discouraged her from acting and even softball, isolating her from her passions and her mother's circle of friends. His Sicilian pride often clashed with Cher's carefree nature, leading to sharp words, like when she excitedly praised new sheets, unknowingly bruising his ego.

Their lives outside the home were just as intense. At Gold Star, Phillip Spector pushed them through grueling sessions for his Christmas album. Sonny worked tirelessly, staying overnight with Phillip, while Cher often stayed home, feeling uneasy. One night, while visiting her friend Josita, Cher experienced a terrifying violation when a drunken man crept into her space. Frozen with fear, she escaped and screamed for help. Though shaken, Cher decided not to tell Sonny, knowing his reaction would be explosive.

Life at Gold Star Studios was a whirlwind, with long hours spent finishing Phillip Spector's Christmas album. Cher loved the camaraderie and creative energy, but it wasn't without its chaos. One day, Leon Russell stumbled into the studio, drunk and staggering. "Hey, Leon, ever heard of decorum?" Phillip quipped. Leon slurred back, "Ever heard of 'Fuck you, Phil'?" The room erupted with laughter, even Phillip joining in before snapping them back to work. Despite the exhaustion, the studio had its charm and camaraderie.

When the album was completed, Phillip flew to New York. Hours later, a call came. Phillip had been thrown off his flight after causing a scene, declaring, "You all look like losers! This plane's not gonna make it!" Too exhausted, Sonny handed Cher the car keys. At LAX, she found Phillip passed out, terrified of flying and drugged out. She coaxed him awake, bought him sunglasses, and calmed him down. After pleading with another airline, she managed to get him home safely.

Then, on November 22, 1963, the world stopped. A call from Phillip shattered their morning. "President Kennedy's been shot in Dallas," Sonny murmured. Cher, stunned, burst into tears. They sat frozen, grieving together. JFK had represented hope, youth, and progress–a leader who resonated with their generation.

As the nation mourned, Phillip's Christmas album flopped; no one could celebrate after such a tragedy. Cher and Sonny stayed glued to the TV, united in sorrow, as the weight of history settled over them and the world.

A LOVE SEALED IN SILVER

When Cher discovered she was unexpectedly pregnant, she and Sonny were caught off guard. They weren't planning for a child, and the timing felt chaotic. Still, there was something comforting in the thought of carrying Sonny's baby. Sonny, though excited, worried about how a child might interfere with their dreams in music.

Tragically, Cher lost the baby at sixteen weeks, an experience that left her shaken. Alone when the pain began, she screamed for help, but it was hours before Sonny returned home to find her sobbing on the floor. He rushed her to the doctor, where the agony of loss became real. Together, they grieved deeply, yet their bond grew stronger through shared sorrow. Within a week, Cher was back at Gold Star, throwing herself into work.

One sunny day in the park, Sonny turned to Cher and quipped, "Don't you think it's time you asked me to marry you?" Laughing, she agreed, and they decided on a unique ceremony. With two silver rings engraved with their names, they exchanged vows in their bathroom. Barefoot and between the shower and mirror, they made promises to each other. "I guess we're married now," Sonny said with a grin before heading to the kitchen to cook spaghetti.

Their life together was full of quirks and challenges. When Cher lost her ring, panic set in until she found it in the spaghetti pan days later. They bought a tiny red MGA car, which Cher learned to drive in the Hollywood Hills, giggling with her sister Gee. Even when the car broke down on Sunset, Cher confidently hot-wired it, earning cheers from onlookers.

In their chaotic and unconventional life, Sonny and Cher found joy, laughter, and an unbreakable partnership, laying the foundation for their future as both a couple and an iconic duo.

CHAPTER 9

THE RISE OF SONNY AND CHER

ROLLING WITH THE STONES

Charlie Greene and Brian Stone were like characters straight out of *Sweet Smell of Success*–fast-talking, sharp, and completely committed to their hustles. Their story was as audacious as their personalities. Starting as teenage press agents in New York, they failed spectacularly, then hitchhiked to LA with only $8 to their names. Once in Hollywood, they brazenly snuck onto the Universal Studios lot, claimed a dressing room as their office, and managed to pass themselves off as legitimate press agents for six months before being caught. Their charm and relentless energy made them magnetic, and people couldn't help but be drawn into their schemes.

Sonny first met them through Gold Star Studios, where they were working on a version of "Yes Sir, That's My Baby." The project, released under the name Hale and the Hushabyes, brought together industry heavyweights like Brian Wilson, Darlene Love, and Jackie DeShannon. Charlie and Brian's ability to pull off something so improbable was a testament to their enthusiasm and unshakable belief in their vision.

At the time, Sonny and Cher were struggling as Caesar & Cleo, playing small gigs at roller rinks and bowling alleys. Meeting Charlie and Brian reignited Sonny's drive. The duo, eager to learn the music industry ropes, struck a deal with Sonny: in exchange for his expertise, they let Sonny and Cher use their office, telephones, and secretary. The partnership created a contagious energy, like a spark meeting dry kindling. Charlie and Brian signed Caesar & Cleo, giving Sonny and Cher a renewed sense of purpose and hope.

Around this time, the Rolling Stones arrived in LA for their first American tour. Sonny, eager to meet them, took Cher to the Hilton where the band was staying. While Sonny stepped away, the band–led by a flirtatious Mick Jagger–spotted Cher alone and struck up a conversation. When Sonny returned, he jokingly wagged his finger, saying, "Hey, you guys, that's my wife!" He then introduced Cher to the group. Nineteen-year-old Mick Jagger was already the star, while Keith Richards came across as sweet and shy. But it was Brian Jones, angelic and striking, who caught Cher's attention.

Though she was thrilled by the encounter, Cher's growing awareness of Sonny's disapproval kept her reserved. A single glance from him could silence her, and she found herself hesitant to speak too freely in his presence.

The Rolling Stones warmed to Sonny and Cher immediately. Unlike the stiff American record executives in suits they had been meeting, Sonny and Cher were relaxed, fun, and relatable. The band wanted to escape the formalities and hang out with people who shared their vibe. When Brian Jones asked if they could stay at Sonny and Cher's place, Sonny was flattered but hesitant, knowing their two-room apartment with no living room furniture wasn't exactly rock-star ready. Embarrassed, he whispered to Cher about the idea of cots. She laughed and said, "Son, c'mon, get real." Sonny explained their situation, and the band stayed at their hotel.

Mick Jagger then invited Sonny and Cher to the band's first American gig at the Swing Auditorium in San Bernardino. Arriving on a school bus provided by the record company, they were stunned by the energy of the crowd. The 3,500 fans—mostly young women—screamed and cheered wildly. Watching from the side of the stage, Sonny and Cher marveled at the chaos and sheer noise.

After the show, the mania escalated as frenzied fans surrounded the bus. One girl handed Cher a pen and paper for Mick's autograph. When she tried to return it, a swarm of hands grabbed at her, almost pulling her out of the window. Sonny had to yank her back inside. In the frenzy, someone pulled the amethyst out of the birthday ring her mother had given her. It was a dreadful lesson in how intense fan obsession could be.

Despite the chaos, Cher and Sonny loved spending time with the Stones. Mick, impressed by Sonny's experience, suggested they try launching their music in Britain: "Trust me, man, they won't be afraid of you there." Inspired, Sonny wrote *Baby Don't Go*, a personal song crafted for Cher, with lyrics reflecting her life struggles and dreams. Both Charlie and Brian loved the song, sparking new hope for Sonny and Cher's future.

THE BIRTH OF SONNY & CHER

By 1964, Sonny, Cher, Charlie Greene, and Brian Stone were inseparable—a team fueled by ambition and infectious energy. To save money, the four moved into a funky Laurel Canyon house with their girlfriends, including Marcie, whose influence encouraged Cher to embrace a touch of glamour. Their shared space became a hub of creativity and collaboration, driving Sonny to pull together musicians for a song he believed in: *Baby Don't Go*.

Harold Battiste, Leon Russell, and others contributed their talents for free, and Sonny coaxed Cher into singing lead despite her nerves. "I can't do this without you," she begged. Sonny joined her on the choruses, their voices locking in perfect harmony.

Eager to test the song, Sonny pitched it to Phillip Spector, offering half the royalties for $500. Phillip paid up, intrigued. Charlie and Brian's relentless enthusiasm drove Sonny to push further. The group barged into Reprise executive Mo Ostin's office to play the track, unaware he didn't recognize them as his own signed artists. Mo loved the song and offered a better deal than their original contract. Sonny and Cher signed it, launching their career as a duo.

Baby Don't Go was released in September 1964 under Frank Sinatra's Reprise label. It became a regional hit, thanks to relentless radio call-ins from friends and family. Buoyed by their momentum, Sonny made a bold decision: it was time to leave Phillip Spector and strike out on their own.

Their final backing session for Spector was on *You've Lost That Lovin' Feelin'* by the Righteous Brothers. As the Wall of Sound filled the studio, everyone stood in awe, knowing they were part of music history. Cher and Sonny left inspired, ready to carve their own path to stardom.

Leaving the rigorous schedules of Gold Star Studios behind, Sonny and Cher found themselves broke but determined. As they navigated a world shifting musically, politically, and culturally, the two became inspired by the burgeoning counterculture in California. Amid this backdrop, Cher's personal style began to evolve, sparked by an encounter with Colleen and Bridget, two young women crafting daring fashion statements. Their bold "elephant bell" pants and vibrant designs inspired Cher to push her boundaries, experimenting with styles that soon became part of her signature look. She also began styling Sonny, encouraging him to embrace eccentric, fearless fashion.

Their defining moment came when a travel mishap forced them to perform in their everyday clothes. Appearing in floral bell-bottoms and striped pants at a gig near San Francisco, they were mistaken for British artists. The audience's enthusiastic response marked a turning point, convincing them to ditch their cheesy costumes and perform as themselves.

With "Baby Don't Go" gaining traction, Sonny and Cher signed with Atlantic Records, and Sonny focused on crafting a song to cement their breakthrough. Late one night in early 1965, Sonny woke Cher to sing a new tune he'd written: *I Got You Babe*. Initially unimpressed,

Cher reluctantly provided feedback, requesting a modulation to add excitement. Sonny reworked the song, and when she finally sang it, the chemistry was undeniable.

They recorded the song at Gold Star Studios, and when Atlantic Records' president Ahmet Ertegun heard it, even Cher's mother chimed in to champion her daughter's talent. Released in the summer of 1965, *I Got You Babe* quickly gained momentum, propelled by DJ Sam Riddle's support. Meanwhile, Sonny and Cher joined the Beach Boys on tour, where their unique look captivated audiences just as much as their music.

As the song climbed the charts, the duo's playful yet sincere chemistry resonated with listeners, cementing their place as icons of the era. It was a whirlwind of sleepless nights, creative sparks, and an unshakable belief in their dream that made *I Got You Babe* a defining anthem of 1965, and Sonny and Cher household names.

THE ROAD TO LONDON

Moving into a house on Hemet Place in Hollywood, Cher was struck by a strange familiarity, as if she'd lived there before. They furnished their new home with essentials, setting up a creative space in the garage where Sonny could write music and where friends Bridget and Colleen could sew unique outfits.

Despite the financial constraints, life was filled with simple pleasures like dining at a local Italian eatery, enjoying pasta for a modest price while observing an eclectic cast of characters.

Sonny's foray into film with "Wild on the Beach" didn't yield commercial success, but it sparked an idea for future projects. Encouraged by British friends, Sonny decided on a bold move. "We're going to London," he declared, proposing they sell everything they owned, from the house to their cars, to fund this adventure. Cher, initially doubtful, was swept up by Sonny's vision for a new chapter across the Atlantic.

To plan their upcoming trip to London, Sonny and Cher met with their managers, Charlie and Brian, over lunch before heading to their office on Sunset and Highland. Upon entering, they found a large man with a prominent mustache sitting in a chair, arms folded and scowling. Charlie and Brian, visibly rattled, quickly ducked into another room, leaving Sonny and Cher to face the visitor. Introducing himself as Joe DeCarlo, the man claimed ties to Frank Sinatra and Jilly Rizzo, as well as managing Louis Prima and Keely Smith. Despite the intimidating start, Sonny's Sicilian charm soon had Joe laughing, and the two retreated to talk in private.

Later that night, Sonny revealed to Cher that Charlie and Brian had borrowed money from the wrong people, and Joe had come to collect—or worse. Sonny, in his usual shrewd way, managed to negotiate a repayment plan in installments. He even secured some advice from Joe, suggesting that if Sonny and Cher became as successful as Louis and Keely, Charlie and Brian could repay the loan faster.

Joe's tough exterior masked an incredible past, which he recounted to Cher in "bedtime stories." From surviving on Iwo Jima during World War II to witnessing the Japanese surrender on the USS Missouri, Joe's experiences fascinated her, whether entirely true or not. He became a father figure to her, and despite his questionable history, she adored him.

By August 1965, Sonny and Cher, along with Gee, Charlie, and Brian, flew to London, dressed in their signature bold styles. Cher wore her iconic red, white, and blue striped bell-bottoms, and Sonny sported his fur vest. Exhausted from the journey, Cher was still groggy from a sleeping pill when they arrived at the Hilton. At the front desk, the receptionist coldly denied their reservation, dismissing them despite Sonny's proof. Feeling humiliated, Cher wanted to cry, but Sonny remained calm, capturing photographic evidence of their booking.

Their dismissal from the Hilton made instant headlines. As reporters swarmed outside, Sonny turned the rejection into a publicity opportunity, ensuring they were photographed and interviewed. Relocating to a shabby prewar hotel with a lumpy bed and barely functioning shower, they collapsed into sleep, determined to face their London adventure with fresh energy.

A DREAM REALIZED

Sonny and Cher arrived in London unsure of their prospects, with no gigs lined up and no plan. Cranky and anxious, they feared their gamble had failed. But by the time they'd bathed and dressed, they were famous. Photos of their Hilton eviction had made headlines, and calls flooded in for interviews and appearances. Everyone was captivated by their unique look. Rumors swirled that the Hilton incident had been a publicity stunt, but Cher dismissed it. "That desk clerk looked at us like dirt. He wasn't that good an actor." Whatever the truth, the publicity worked wonders. The hotel later hosted a press conference to apologize, cementing the duo's newfound fame.

Their song *I Got You Babe* soared to the top of the UK charts, staying there for two weeks, followed by their earlier singles. They performed on *Top of the Pops* and *Ready Steady Go!* and posed for countless photos. In London, their eccentric style wasn't mocked but celebrated. Cher recalled signing her first British autograph for a sweet old lady in a tobacco shop. The moment was surreal.

London embraced them. By day, they shopped Carnaby Street and Chelsea's King's Road, picking up bespoke Beatle boots, paisley bell-bottoms, and a rabbit-fur coat that left Cher skipping with joy. By night, they partied at the Ad Lib Club and Scotch of St. James, meeting icons like the Rolling Stones, Dusty Springfield, and John Lennon. The excitement was intoxicating.

Despite the whirlwind, Cher admitted exhaustion. Crowds grew overwhelming, especially at record store appearances where security often failed to hold back frenzied fans. Still, they were grateful. Cher reflected, "We'd only dreamed of this. Sonny called me his missing piece, and I felt the same about him."

When *I Got You Babe* knocked the Beatles' *Help!* off the top spot, selling a million copies in two weeks, their dream had truly come to life. As their earlier singles climbed the charts, they became one of the only acts besides Elvis and the Beatles to have five songs in the UK top twenty simultaneously. Cher marveled, "We entered London unknown. We left as Sonny & Cher, known the world over."

Returning to America as stars, they left London on a high, grateful for their British fans and the magical success of a song that would define their careers. As Cher drifted off on the plane, she whispered to Sonny, "Wake me when we land–and get me a burger."

CHAPTER 10

STARDOM AND STRUGGLES

FROM NEW YORK TO THE ED SULLIVAN SPOTLIGHT

Landing at John F. Kennedy Airport, Sonny and Cher were greeted by a surreal scene: five thousand screaming teenagers holding banners, rushing toward them. Startled, Cher froze, nearly fleeing until police and fire crews helped them escape into a waiting limousine. The chaotic reception was a sign that their British success had crossed the Atlantic, though some mistook them for a British Invasion band.

Settling into the Hampshire House Hotel in Manhattan, Cher marveled at how far she'd come. The wild teenager living in New York with her mom and stepdad was now a star. Atlantic Records president Ahmet Ertegun welcomed them back with open arms, inviting them to his legendary Upper East Side parties. There, they mingled with luminaries like Andy Warhol and Baby Jane Holzer. Cher struck up a friendship with Ahmet's wife, Mica, who once hilariously mistook a joint for a shared cigarette among broke musicians.

With newfound fame came relentless work. They returned to the studio to finish *Look at Us*, enlisting Gold Star musicians to record covers like "Unchained Melody." Meanwhile, Cher's solo album *All I Really Want to Do* climbed the charts. As their fame soared, Freddy Apollo of the William Morris Agency signed them, though he initially doubted their eccentric image.

Sonny and Cher's star was rising fast when they were invited to perform on NBC's *Hullabaloo*, hosted by Sammy Davis Jr. Sharing the stage with the Supremes and the Lovin' Spoonful, they performed "Babe" and the Rolling Stones' "(I Can't Get No) Satisfaction." The show closed with a quirky group performance of "I'm Henry VIII, I Am" alongside Sammy, who struck up a friendship with Sonny over their shared love of photography.

Soon after, the duo received a career-defining invitation to appear on CBS's *The Ed Sullivan Show*, the biggest television show in America, watched by an audience of seventy million. For Cher, the opportunity was overwhelming—this was the same stage where Elvis and the Beatles had performed. Sonny and Cher arrived for rehearsals nervous but excited, knowing this was proof they'd truly "arrived."

Ed Sullivan himself, famously powerful and influential, kept his distance, watching them rehearse with his arms crossed. His glowing introduction during the live broadcast, calling them "two fine youngsters" and lauding their success, was somewhat marred by his repeated mispronunciation of Cher's name as "Chur."

Despite this, they gave a spirited performance, opening with "I Got You Babe." Cher followed with "Where Do You Go," and they closed with Sonny's "But You're Mine." In hindsight, Cher questioned why they didn't perform their hits like "Baby Don't Go," which could have capitalized on the enormous audience. Instead, Sonny used the moment to showcase his songwriting.

Their time on *The Ed Sullivan Show* was brief but unforgettable, cementing Sonny and Cher's status as sensations. Even with Sullivan's blunders, the experience marked a monumental milestone in their journey.

FAME, FASHION, AND FREEDOM

Sonny relentlessly packed their schedule, capitalizing on their growing fame. Cher enjoyed TV appearances, like *Hollywood Palace*, where Milton Berle hilariously pretended to be their child. However, the grueling workload took its toll. Overworked, Cher fell ill after a vaccination became infected. "It's too much," she begged Sonny, but he remained focused on their career. Despite the chaos, Cher found joy in designing a Sonny & Cher fashion line, which sold out immediately. The collection, full of their signature unisex vests and elephant bells, excluded miniskirts due to Sonny's disapproval, though Cher cleverly found ways to wear them.

Teen fans swarmed their Encino home after a magazine article revealed its location. Sonny welcomed them, often inviting them in for heart-to-heart talks. Cher was overwhelmed by the attention, even writing a "Dear Cher" column for *Teen Beat.* Although she started answering letters herself, the workload soon passed to the magazine staff, leaving her feeling disconnected from her young fans.

One fan, Joey, became a regular visitor and close friend, joining Cher on shopping trips and forming a lifelong bond. The only freedom Sonny allowed Cher was solo shopping excursions, a brief respite from their demanding life. During one outing, Cher spotted a pricey Rudi Gernreich pantsuit but faced dismissive treatment from a snooty saleswoman. Determined, she bought the suit in every color to prove her worth but left the store in tears. Sonny reassured her, "It doesn't matter. Come home."

Despite the pressures, Cher found solace in moments of independence and the love she shared with Sonny.

In late 1965, Cher and Sonny received a surprising invitation: perform at a Manhattan soirée hosted by millionaires Charles and Jane Engelhard, with Jacqueline Kennedy as the guest of honor. Jackie, a fan of "I Got You Babe," had requested their presence. Arriving at the Waldorf Astoria, they rehearsed in a luxurious apartment adorned with platinum ornaments. Nervously, Cher wore a green velvet military-style outfit and Beatle boots while Sonny stuck to his signature vest.

After their performance, staff hurried to usher them out, but Jackie intervened. "Where are Sonny and Cher? I want to speak with them." Brought back in, they joined Jackie for dessert. Cher, seated beside the elegant former First Lady, nervously asked, "How are Caroline and John Junior?" Jackie's warmth put her at ease. Sonny gifted Jackie saint medals for her children, earning her admiration as she playfully called him "Shakespearean."

The evening marked a turning point for Cher. Diana Vreeland, the legendary *Vogue* editor, noticed her at the party and later invited her for a photoshoot with renowned photographer Richard Avedon. During the session, Cher was skittish but mesmerized by Avedon's charm and ease. Diana praised Cher as "divine," marveling at her unique look. "She's the new woman," Diana declared.

Avedon's talent helped Cher feel truly beautiful for the first time. He captured her in striking, unconventional poses, including a backless shot that made her anxious about Sonny's reaction. Diana, ever the strategist, charmed Sonny with glowing praise for Cher and the artistry of the photos. He was won over before seeing the images.

The shoot sparked Cher's transformation. She felt free, creative, and seen in a way she hadn't before. Though Avedon doubted she'd ever make the cover of *Vogue*, Cher proved him wrong six years later, a milestone he graciously celebrated. That night and the shoot that followed became defining moments in Cher's journey, propelling her from self-doubt to confidence and stardom.

RISING FAME, TUMBLING FORTUNES

In November 1965, Princess Margaret and her husband, Lord Snowdon, invited Sonny and Cher to perform at the Hollywood Palladium. Known for their rising fame among the younger generation, the duo was surprised by the invitation, as the event was geared toward the old Hollywood elite who hardly understood their style or appeal. Despite their reluctance, they couldn't refuse an invitation from British royalty. Unfortunately, the performance was a disaster. The event started late, sound issues plagued the night, and halfway through their set, Princess Margaret asked for the volume to be lowered due to a headache. The audience's polite applause barely masked their indifference, and critic Peter Bogdanovich later described their performance as "howling like coyotes." The ordeal was humiliating, but Sonny and Cher persevered, knowing the entertainment industry was filled with such ups and downs.

Bogdanovich spent three days with Sonny and Cher to write a profile for *The Saturday Evening Post*. Though intended to highlight their success, the resulting article painted Cher in an unflattering light, misrepresenting her compassion as disdain during an encounter with a disabled person and including offhand remarks about her mother that she hadn't meant seriously. To make matters worse, the article included their home address, inviting fans to invade their privacy. Sonny was livid, declaring Cher off-limits for future interviews—a decision she welcomed, retreating further into the background while Sonny managed their public image.

By January 1966, their career saw a brighter moment when Sonny and Cher headlined at the Hollywood Bowl, selling out in just 24 hours. Sharing the stage with acts like the Righteous Brothers and the Mamas & the Papas, the performance was electric. Fans rushed the stage during "I Got You Babe," but Cher's cool-headed plea for calm worked, and the night ended on a triumphant note. It was a moment of pride for Cher's family, including her grandfather, who told her mother, "That's you up on that stage, Jackie Jean. It's you!"

However, fame brought chaos, too. At a San Francisco concert, fans stormed the stage, and Cher was mistaken for one of them by a security guard who put her in a headlock, leaving her shaken. Ready to quit, Sonny convinced her to keep going, promising things would get better. As a gesture of comfort, he took her to Sausalito for a carefree day, a brief respite from the pressures of fame.

Despite the turbulence, Sonny and Cher's influence on youth culture was undeniable. Girls mimicked Cher's Cleopatra eyeliner and sleek hair, while boys adopted Sonny's bohemian style. Cher, reflecting on the growing adoration, marveled at how far they'd come from being an unknown act. Witnessing such idolization reminded her of the first time she saw Tina Turner backstage, a whirlwind of charisma and power. Like Tina, Cher was discovering the unique force she and Sonny brought to the world.

FROM STARDOM TO VOGUE

Back in LA, Sonny and Cher temporarily moved in with her mother while searching for a permanent place. Advised to buy instead of rent, they toured a $75,000 show home on Academia Drive in Encino and bought it instantly. The single-story house boasted a spacious living room, enormous closets, a luxurious bathroom, and a swimming pool overlooking the Valley. They purchased the house fully furnished, with interior design by Ronnie Wilson, whom Cher admired for his flair and metallic-blue Corvette.

Meanwhile, Cher's mother and sister, Gee, moved into a nearby rental, supported financially by Sonny, though Cher was never sure how much he gave them. Despite their newfound success, Cher harbored insecurities about losing everything, a fear rooted in her modest childhood. She began hoarding duplicate items–two hair dryers, two frying pans–as a safeguard against scarcity.

Life in their new home was far from restful. Sonny's relentless drive left little room for leisure. They rarely went out, avoided vacations, and Cher wasn't allowed to see friends without him. "This is our time," Sonny would say, reminding her of fame's fleeting nature. But Cher struggled with the pace and isolation.

Sonny wasn't one for nightlife, but when he occasionally took Cher to clubs, it wasn't for dancing–it was to network. Cher, feeling restricted, couldn't even wear perfume or listen to music without Sonny's approval. "Anything we can't do together isn't worth doing," he'd say, a philosophy that quietly eroded her sense of self. Yet she didn't notice how much of herself she was losing, becoming a shadow of the vibrant person Sonny first admired.

Despite their rising fame, Sonny's missteps began alienating fans. His anti-drug PSA, condemning marijuana during the counterculture era, made them seem out of touch. Cher privately disagreed with his stance, knowing it would alienate younger audiences. The fallout was swift: record sales plummeted, and their agency downgraded them to less prestigious bookings.

Behind the scenes, Sonny's mood darkened. Cher sensed prescription meds might be involved, and his relentless drive only intensified. For Christmas, she gifted him twelve leather-bound journals, hoping they might offer him clarity. Sonny wrote prolifically, often waking Cher in the middle of the night to share his musings. The journals became their unconventional way of communicating, with Cher occasionally leaving notes for him to find.

Years later, Cher discovered an entry Sonny had written on his 33rd birthday: *"I am never sans Cher. She lives inside my body. Cher is truly a star from the top of her head to the bottom of her feet. Thank God I have Cher. She is my stabilizer. She is my generator too. She's my reason."* Cher was stunned, wishing she'd known how deeply he felt.

Even amid rising challenges, their bond remained the anchor of their whirlwind lives, though the cracks in their partnership were beginning to show.

CHAPTER 11

THE RISE, FALL, AND RESILIENCE

SONNY'S FILMMAKING DREAM

Sonny, always looking ahead, decided to make a movie starring himself and Cher. "It'll be like the Beatles' films, only better," he declared, bragging to his poker buddies, including Francis Ford Coppola and Billy Friedkin. Frustrated by his endless chatter, they finally said, "Then make it yourself!" Motivated, Sonny hired Billy, an aspiring director in his twenties, and took over the screenplay after firing the original writer, holding late-night "writers' conferences" to finalize ideas.

Cher, wary of the film's campy premise, reluctantly went along. Sonny called in favors, getting Harold Battiste to arrange the score, including a jazzy version of "I Got You Babe." Paramount eventually backed the project, and Sonny titled it *Good Times*. The movie was a comedic musical filled with skits spoofing films like *The Maltese Falcon* and *High Noon*, featuring Sonny as a gullible singer manipulated by a shady producer, while Cher played the skeptical wife.

The set buzzed with activity. Cher felt self-conscious, having recently gained weight, but she was thrilled to meet actor George Sanders, who charmed her with his wit and introduced her to the term déjà vu. Much of the movie was filmed at Africa USA, a wildlife park. Cher grew close to an elephant named Margie, who let her ride on her back. But a tiger's rough lick on her leg and fears of hidden alligators in a lake kept her on edge.

Sonny's dream turned real, with their personalized Mustangs featured in the film. The comedic, corny *Good Times* may not have been a masterpiece, but it marked Sonny's bold step into filmmaking and cemented their unique style on screen.

Whenever Sonny hit a low point, he turned to writing. Desperate for a new direction and a steady revenue stream, he became consumed with his next project, a film he planned to call *Chastity*. The story followed a homeless young woman hitchhiking across the country in search of meaning, a concept Sonny believed would reconnect them to the youth culture of the time. His passion for the film grew after Billy Friedkin called to urge him, "You *must* come and see this new movie!" That film was *The Graduate*, starring Dustin Hoffman and Anne Bancroft. Inspired and awestruck, Sonny secretly aspired to create something equally groundbreaking.

To finalize *Chastity*, Sonny hired a young, blonde secretary to take dictation. One night, Cher awoke thirsty and wandered barefoot through their open-plan house toward the kitchen. As she passed the den, she noticed two shadowy figures behind the wrought-iron gate. Still groggy, she didn't think much of it until she heard whispering and rustling noises. On her way back to the bedroom, she caught sight of Sonny helping his "assistant" out the front door. It was such a cliché, and her heart broke.

Cher went straight to bed, lying on the very edge. When Sonny tried to speak, she cut him off sharply: "Don't say a word." Somehow, she managed to sleep. In the early hours of the morning, she packed a bag and left for her mother's house.

Her mother, livid upon hearing what had happened, didn't hold back. "Cher, honey, I've been hearing stories about him for a while now," she said. But Cher, overwhelmed with sadness, couldn't bear to hear more. Sonny later called to plead his case, blaming her for not having enough sex with him. His words stung, but his charm was disarming, and by the end of the conversation, Cher found herself apologizing.

The incident drove a wedge between Sonny and Cher's mother. Her mother eventually wrote Cher a letter listing her grievances, and for a time, she stopped speaking to her entirely.

BURNING BRIDGES AND BROKEN DREAMS

In the summer of 1967, Cher became pregnant again, but her joy was short-lived. While shopping with Joey in Hollywood, she doubled over in pain, realizing she was losing the baby. Making it home before the worst began, she endured another devastating miscarriage, her second in a year. "I don't want to do this anymore," she tearfully told Sonny, confiding in her gynecologist, who diagnosed her with an "angry uterus." The news crushed her, leaving her doubting if she'd ever be a mother.

Sonny and Cher's life took an exciting turn when they attended a birthday party hosted by Tony Curtis at his Italian Renaissance mansion in Holmby Hills. The star of *Some Like It Hot* and *Spartacus*, Curtis was renowned for his extravagant lifestyle and love of surrounding himself with "hip" people. Though they had never met him, Sonny and Cher found themselves among the glittering crowd of celebrities at his lavish celebration.

As Sonny drove them up the long driveway, Cher was stunned by the grandeur of the estate. The massive property, with its sprawling manicured lawns, frescoed ceilings, and ornate marble fireplaces, seemed like something out of a movie. The mansion boasted nine bedrooms, ten bathrooms, an Olympic-sized swimming pool, stables, and even a secret door in the screening room–rumored to have been installed for Marilyn Monroe's discreet visits to its former owner, Twentieth Century–Fox founder Joseph Schenck.

Walking through the opulent home, Cher was captivated. "We're going to live here one day," she declared to Sonny. He laughed at her ambition but didn't dismiss her dream.

Tony Curtis greeted them warmly, his black velvet suit and silk scarf adding to his theatrical charm. When Cher gushed over his house, he revealed that he had moved out months ago and invited them to see his other property, a smaller version of the mansion, now up for sale.

A few days later, they visited 364 St. Cloud Road in Bel-Air. The elegant home mirrored the grandeur of the Holmby Hills mansion but on a more intimate scale. Cher fell in love with it instantly, exploring its billiards room, paneled library, six bedrooms, and expansive pool. Seeing her excitement, Sonny turned to Tony and said he wished he could buy it for her. "For you, daahling, just two hundred fifty thousand dollars," Curtis replied with a flourish.

On the drive home, Cher whispered, "Son..." Sonny sighed but nodded. "All right. We'll swing it."

Within weeks, Tony allowed them to move in, even though Sonny hadn't yet secured the funds. It was a dream come true for Cher. They invited friends and family over for a barbecue, and everyone marveled at the grandeur of their new home. For Cher, it felt like a fairy tale had come to life.

Once Sonny and Cher moved into their new home, Sonny confessed he'd spent all their money and couldn't afford furniture. Their grand house remained largely bare, save for a four-poster canopy bed, a mahogany dining table, and a sunroom lovingly decorated by Ronnie Wilson. Despite the sparse furnishings, Cher was thrilled, seeing the house as a dream realized.

However, cracks in their relationship began to widen. One night, after watching *The Dirty Dozen*, Sonny accused Cher of liking the movie because she was "sexually frustrated." Stunned, she protested, but Sonny erupted. "Pull over! Let me out!" he shouted. Frightened, Cher stopped the car, and Sonny stormed off into the darkness. Denis Pregnolato rescued him, but Sonny returned home furious, yelling, "How dare you leave me there?" before storming out again. Cher was left shaken and confused.

Hoping to find some balance, Cher confided in Joe DeCarlo about her need for an outlet. With his help, she began tennis lessons, relishing the physical activity and sense of freedom. But when Sonny learned she'd spoken to men at her coach's party, he burned her tennis clothes in the backyard. Watching the flames, Cher felt an overwhelming mix of anger and despair. Something shifted within her that night.

Meanwhile, Sonny poured everything into his new film, *Chastity*. Unable to secure studio backing, he took out loans and gathered a small crew to shoot the story of a wandering, troubled girl. Cher, wearing her own clothes, played the titular role, a character Sonny claimed was inspired by her. On set, she bonded with British actor Stephen Whittaker, a fellow dreamer who gave her a rare sense of camaraderie. For Cher, it was a brief solace amid an increasingly tumultuous life.

MARRIAGE AND WORK COLLIDE

In the early hours of June 6, 1968, Sonny received a phone call that brought everything to a halt. Robert Kennedy had been assassinated at the Ambassador Hotel in Los Angeles. At just forty-two years old, Kennedy had recently won the Democratic presidential primary. The news shook Sonny and Cher deeply. Although they had only met Kennedy a few times, his charm and vision had left a lasting impression. They had planned to campaign for him after completing *Chastity*. His death, coming just two months after Martin Luther King Jr.'s assassination, felt like yet another devastating loss for the country.

Shortly after, Sonny and Cher performed at the Soul Together concert at Madison Square Garden, a benefit for a fund in Martin Luther King Jr.'s name. Sharing the stage with legends like Aretha Franklin, Jimi Hendrix, and Sam & Dave, they felt honored to be part of such a historic event. Cher, dressed in a pale pink satin gown of her own design, had a memorable encounter with Hendrix backstage. Despite his reputation, Jimi was polite and charismatic, leaving a lasting impression on Cher. Tragically, his death two years later would add his name to the growing list of musicians lost to the excesses of the era.

After the concert, Sonny and Cher returned to Arizona to resume filming *Chastity*. Sonny's jealousy and controlling nature surfaced on set when he rearranged Cher's schedule to limit her interaction with her co-star, Stephen. This possessiveness disrupted the creative flow and compromised the film's storyline, turning an already disjointed script into something even harder to follow.

As filming wrapped, Cher discovered she was pregnant again. Her doctor prescribed bed rest, much to Sonny's dismay, as their finances were stretched thin. Sonny continued working tirelessly, attending the Democratic National Convention and pitching political ideas. However, his tone-deaf decisions, including a government-sponsored film warning teens about marijuana, painted him as out of touch. Cher, meanwhile, tried to find solace in her pregnancy and much-needed rest after years of turmoil and creative struggles.

THE BIRTH OF CHASTITY SUN

Sonny's erratic behavior often left Cher confused, though she never suspected he might secretly be taking drugs. Known for his staunchly anti-drug stance, it seemed unthinkable. However, one day, while resting in their bedroom, Cher witnessed their bodyguard, Big Jim, place something in Sonny's bathroom cabinet. Curious, she later checked and found a large white plastic bottle filled with hundreds of Valium pills. This discovery shocked her. Sonny's private bathroom had always been off-limits, and she hadn't realized he was using the pills to manage pain from his kidney stones. His mood swings, unpredictable nights, and constant restlessness suddenly made more sense.

Amid this turmoil, Sonny abruptly called Cher from his office one day and announced, "I'm coming home, and we're getting married." For Cher, who already considered them married since their informal ring exchange, the ceremony was a mere formality. The wedding was quick and secretive, attended only by their lawyer and two witnesses. There was no dress, cake, or celebration–just a legal document to protect their public image in an era when living together before marriage was scandalous. Despite the rushed nature of the event, Cher felt no resentment. She was content knowing they were officially married, carrying Sonny's child, and continuing their life together. The moment was understated, yet meaningful in its own way.

In early 1969, Cher was overjoyed when her pregnancy progressed without complications. Sonny, eager for a boy, took countless photos of her growing belly, teasing her with, "Remember, I want a boy!" Cher only wished for a healthy baby. As her due date neared, their excitement strengthened their bond. At her baby shower, surrounded by friends like Cass Elliot and Liza Minnelli, the reality of impending motherhood finally hit Cher as she held up tiny rompers and booties.

On March 3, Cher's contractions began in earnest. Calling Sonny, she cried, "This is it!" but he assumed it was another false alarm. It was only Joe D's insistence that made Sonny rush to Cedars-Sinai, where he greeted Cher with a camera, snapping photos as she laughed through her panic. "I'll kill you if you don't stop taking pictures!" she warned, half-smiling.

Labor was terrifying. With no epidural available, Cher relied on her gynecologist, Dr. Heldfond, and his compassionate nurse, Elizabeth, for comfort. In the early hours, Cher heard her baby's first cry. Overwhelmed with relief, she repeatedly asked, "Does my baby have all its fingers and toes?" before exhaustion overtook her. The next morning, Sonny revealed they had a seven-pound-eight-ounce baby girl. Cher named her Chastity Sun, combining her *Chastity* film character with Sonny's nickname.

Joy turned to fear when Chastity was kept in an incubator to stabilize her temperature. Sonny's anger at the hospital staff was palpable, but relief came when they brought Chastity home. However, Cher's first night back was marred by a hemorrhage that left her faint and weak. Sonny found her collapsed and stayed by her side, calling the doctor and nursing her back to health.

When Cher's mother finally visited months later, she criticized Chastity as "insecure," sparking Sonny's fury. Despite the chaos, Cher found strength in her new role as a mother, vowing to give Chastity the love and security she deserved. Holding her baby close, Cher knew this was her purpose, determined to grow into motherhood, no matter what challenges lay ahead.

CHAPTER 12

THE COMEBACK COUPLE

THE FIRST COMEBACK

By late 1969, Sonny and Cher were struggling.

Cher had recorded her sixth solo album, *3614 Jackson Highway*, at the famed Muscle Shoals studio. Despite Jerry Wexler's legendary production, Sonny's interference strained the process. Cher found solace lying in a nearby cemetery, jokingly "talking to the dead guys." Though Sonny praised the album as her best, it failed commercially.

June 1969 also saw the release of *Chastity*, their passion project. Rated R unnecessarily, it alienated their target audience and flopped. Critics panned it, leaving Cher and Sonny disheartened. Sick with the flu, they skipped the premiere, marking yet another setback in their tumultuous journey.

With no hit records or movies, their planned concert tour was canceled, and their agent Harvey Kresky left for more successful clients. Desperate to stay afloat, Sonny sold their house and booked them into supper clubs and dinner theaters. It wasn't glamorous, but it was work. They packed Chastity in a travel crib and, with their sweet new nanny Heidi, set out for Windsor, Ontario, to perform at the Elmwood Casino.

Their first stay was far from luxurious. The motel across from the casino had mildew-covered walls and faulty plumbing, and passing trains kept them awake all night. To save money, Sonny cooked pasta sauce for the band on a hot plate in their room. Despite the dreary circumstances, Sonny insisted Cher adopt a more sophisticated stage look. She donned a Grecian-style dress with bronze chains and Roman sandals, exuding elegance even as they navigated greasy kitchen floors en route to tiny audiences.

Their crowds, once thousands of screaming fans, dwindled to fewer than a hundred. One midnight show had only four people in the audience. Cher's nerves often overwhelmed her. "I can't do it," she told Sonny, panicked. Sonny reassured her, "Just come for the opening and leave if you need to." His calm encouragement got her through each show, even as they sang to indifferent diners.

Determined to stay visible, Sonny arranged TV appearances. On *The Mike Douglas Show*, Sonny confidently explained their supper club gigs. "It solidifies you as a performer," he said. Privately, he dreamed of pushing Cher forward as a solo star, a plan that would slowly take root in their uphill battle for relevance.

Three weeks after Chastity's birth, she made her first television appearance, bringing some light into a dark time. For two years, Sonny and Cher's lives revolved around constant gigs in supper clubs, living out of motels. Chastity was their joy. Her milestones—crawling, sitting up—happened on the road, and everyone adored her. Her little blond hair with black tips made her look like a tiny punk rocker, and she would mimic the band, "conducting" rehearsals. Those moments kept them afloat.

Determined to keep their act fresh, Sonny pushed Cher to perform *"Un bel dì"* from *Madame Butterfly* mid-act. "It'll be different," he insisted. Cher reluctantly agreed, but audiences stared, baffled. Ironically, the night they dropped it, someone requested it.

The gigs were grueling. At one midnight show in Windsor, Ontario, Cher finally snapped. Frustrated by an indifferent crowd, she turned her back on them, joking with the band. A heckler yelled, and she snapped back, earning some laughter. Sonny, instead of intervening, let her roll with it. That night, they began to find a new rhythm, connecting with audiences through humor and banter. It wasn't always successful, but it was a start.

One evening, a handwriting analyst in their group told Cher, "You're unhappy. You won't stay with your husband forever." His words haunted her. Days later, she admitted her sadness to Sonny, who exploded. "Do you want me to divorce you?" he shouted. Stunned, Cher resolved never to share her feelings with him again.

FINDING THEIR RHYTHM

Necessity, as they say, became the mother of invention for Sonny and Cher. With their music no longer drawing crowds, they began experimenting with humor on stage. Their banter, initially improvised, evolved into a dynamic that audiences couldn't get enough of. Sonny encouraged Cher to poke fun at him, and she obliged, making jokes about his height, singing, and even his dreams of being a sex symbol. "You'd have to come out naked and on fire to attract attention," she quipped, adding after a beat, "Well, maybe just on fire." Sonny played along, his quick wit and willingness to laugh at himself making him the perfect comedic foil.

As their act grew sharper, their performances began to sell out. The laughter and connection revitalized their energy, transforming their relationship on stage. Sonny's charm and Cher's quick humor found a balance, creating a show that blended music and comedy. Audiences came for the jokes but stayed for the music, and soon, they were gaining traction again.

In the midst of their grueling schedule, they celebrated Chastity's first birthday, finding joy in Sonny's whimsical fairy tales and moments as a father. Though the road was exhausting, their bond deepened as they shared intimate, silly moments with their daughter.

Their hard work began to pay off. Freddy Apollo from William Morris Agency noticed their act and secured them a television special, *The Sonny & Cher Nitty Gritty Hour*. While the show didn't lead to immediate success, it kept them moving forward. They also appeared in *Love, American Style*, a small role that hinted at brighter opportunities.

Then, in June 1971, nearly two years after Sonny's promise to Cher–"Just give me two years, and we'll be back on top"–everything changed. Their perseverance and reinvention finally began to yield the success they so desperately needed.

Fred Silverman, a young programming executive at CBS, discovered Sonny and Cher during a New York performance at the Royal Box supper club. Intrigued, he invited them to guest host *The Merv Griffin Show*. The opportunity was huge; hosting a prime-time talk show was uncharted territory for the couple. Though nervous, they charmed audiences with their interviews, including sessions with Cosmopolitan editor Helen Gurley Brown and actor Michael Blodgett. The show's positive reception planted the seed for something bigger.

Silverman, seeking a contemporary variety show, sent producers Allan Blye and Chris Bearde to evaluate their act at the Fairmont Hotel's Venetian Room. Despite joking about the setting resembling the Titanic, the producers found their dynamic compelling. "As singers they were okay, but as comics they were hysterical," they later admitted. Backstage, they hit it off with Sonny and Cher, and soon a pilot for *The Sonny & Cher Comedy Hour* was in development.

As CBS negotiated contracts, Sonny recalled a lawyer he'd admired, Irwin Spiegel, to handle legalities. Meanwhile, Cher insisted on legendary designer Bob Mackie for her costumes. Despite initial resistance, she secured his collaboration alongside Ret Turner, marking the beginning of a creative partnership.

Filming the pilot at CBS Television City felt surreal after years of struggle. While Sonny fretted, Cher felt ready, supported by a professional crew and their honed routine. The live audience, lured with promises of free food, witnessed a polished act that combined their signature humor with music. Their chemistry clicked, and even Life magazine reporters were present to capture the moment.

Fred Silverman watched from the wings, holding Chastity, his approval vital to their success. The stakes were high, but the night's performance marked the turning point, setting the stage for their rise to television stardom.

REBIRTH

When the announcer's voice boomed, "Ladies and gentlemen, Sonny and Cher!" it marked the beginning of something extraordinary. Standing under the bright lights, Cher realized, *This is it—this is what I'm meant to do.* As the stage wall, adorned with oversized cartoon versions of their faces, lifted, Sonny and Cher emerged, hand in hand. In matching white outfits, they began their signature duet, "The Beat Goes On." Cher playfully took over, forcing Sonny to interrupt, "What am I, chopped liver?" Cher retorted with a knowing smile, "Was," setting the audience roaring with laughter.

Their dynamic carried the show, blending humor and music effortlessly. Sonny's straight-man act complemented Cher's sharp wit, creating an energy audiences couldn't resist. "She's the mother of my child!" Sonny exclaimed during a comedic interruption. Their banter was fresh, their chemistry undeniable.

Guest Jimmy Durante joined in the fun with their "vamp" skits, where Cher portrayed historical women like Cleopatra and Pocahontas, singing and acting with flair. The sketches quickly became fan favorites, showcasing Cher's comedic and theatrical talents.

Fred Silverman, CBS's programming head, believed in them and pushed for their success. Behind the scenes, rehearsals were grueling but rewarding. Cher helped Sonny refine his style, urging him to abandon rigid reliance on cue cards. "Just blow it out and be silly," she told him, and he did, embracing his freewheeling humor.

The show wasn't just work; it was a family affair. Their young daughter, Chastity, thought the set was a playground where everyone dressed up for fun. British nanny Linda Koot ensured Chas was always nearby, bringing joy during long days of filming.

Sketches like "the launderette" and "Mr. and Ms." took shape under the guidance of producers Allan Blye and Chris Bearde. The team worked tirelessly, experimenting with material to perfect the show's blend of comedy, music, and charm.

Though Cher struggled with her hair and makeup under the demanding studio lights, the glowing reviews lifted her spirits. Critics praised their unique chemistry and fresh approach. As Fred Silverman said, “They were very in love and very close,” a bond that shone through in every episode. Sonny’s dream of lasting success seemed within reach. Together, they were creating magic.

The Sonny & Cher Comedy Hour flourished as they navigated grueling schedules filled with rehearsals, costume fittings, and filming. Weekends brought respite, often spent with Chastity at the beach, where a tender moment with her daughter deeply moved Cher. By fall 1971, CBS renewed the show for 13 episodes, attracting talents like Steve Martin and Teri Garr, who became close friends.

Cher’s dazzling costumes became iconic, with viewers tuning in as much for her fashion as the comedy. Alone onstage in Bob Mackie’s creations, she sang classic solos, her confidence bolstered by Sonny’s watchful support. Their dynamic shone, blending playful banter with heartfelt moments.

The show’s success skyrocketed, welcoming stars like Elton John, Tina Turner, and Muhammad Ali. Cher’s quick wit stole scenes, as in jokes about Sonny’s height: “Do you believe in reincarnation?” she’d ask, pausing before quipping, “Then come back taller.”

Backstage, camaraderie flourished while her home life remained grounded. After long days, Cher returned to Chastity, cherishing her role as a mother. Though the demands were immense, the show brought joy, fame, and a renewed sense of purpose, cementing Sonny and Cher as television’s beloved duo.

THE GRIND BEHIND THE GLAMOR

Sonny’s drive to capitalize on their resurgence kept Cher busier than ever. “We have to make the most of this second chance,” he insisted. It wasn’t a suggestion; it was a plan. He sent Cher to record her seventh album, *Chér*, with producer Snuff Garrett, giving her just one week to finish it. Snuffy, a natural comic and efficient producer, clicked with Cher immediately. “Get it done” was his mantra, and Cher rose to the challenge, nailing her vocals quickly with little room for retakes.

The album’s lead single, “Gypsys, Tramps and Thieves,” became Cher’s first solo top-ten hit and earned her a Grammy nomination. Cher fought for Richard Avedon’s striking cover photo, though few supported her choice. The album was so successful it was reissued and renamed after the hit single, eventually going gold. Despite the accolades, Cher barely had time to celebrate. “When you’re juggling an album, TV show, concerts, and motherhood, everything blurs,” she admitted.

Meanwhile, Sonny packed their schedules tight, balancing their TV show with a grueling concert tour of fifty performances by year’s end. Some weeks, they filmed two episodes in three days to make room for nine-day tours. The frenetic pace exhausted Cher, but Sonny’s relentless ambition pushed them forward. As their dear friend George Schlatter joked, “If Sonny and Cher were driving into Hollywood, Sonny would take a gig on Mulholland to break up the trip.” It was relentless, but it was working.

CHAPTER 13

THE RISE AND STRAIN OF STARDOM

The success of *The Sonny & Cher Comedy Hour* brought fame and fortune like never before, but it also strained Sonny and Cher's relationship. Their dynamic on the show flourished–Sonny the lovable fool, Cher the glamorous wit–but their personal lives began to feel hollow. With the IRS debt paid off and a growing wardrobe budget, Cher reveled in her newfound recognition, donning Bob Mackie's dazzling, often risqué designs. "You're on television now, honey," Ret Turner reminded her when fans swarmed at Saks Fifth Avenue. Fame had a different intensity in the TV era, and Cher embraced it, becoming a style icon and earning a spot on America's best-dressed list.

Behind the scenes, though, Sonny's relentless drive to solidify their success wore on Cher. "We have to make the most of this second chance," he insisted, filling their schedules with more gigs, recordings, and appearances. Cher juggled it all with grace, but she began to miss the carefree Sonny she'd first fallen for. His growing obsession with deals, contracts, and cigarillos made him seem more like a "suit" than the man who once cooked pasta sauce with Chas on his hip.

At home, tension simmered. Cher longed for meaningful conversations and freedom to voice her opinions. A casual comment about women's rights turned into a heated argument, leaving her feeling silenced and defeated. "I never fought back," she admitted. "You learn it's not worth it."

Despite the cracks, work remained their refuge. On set, their chemistry and humor enchanted millions. Offstage, Cher found solace in Chas, her love of fashion, and fleeting moments of peace. But as the pressures of fame mounted, Cher couldn't ignore the growing distance between her and Sonny. Their professional success couldn't mask the unraveling of their personal bond.

Cher's dream of living in Tony Curtis's Holmby Hills mansion came true, though not without persistence. "We're going to live in this house one day," she had told Sonny years earlier, and now it symbolized their triumph. "Please, Sonny, can we buy it?" she pleaded, tears in her eyes. Sonny rarely said no to Cher's rare requests, and soon they moved into the 12,200-square-foot mansion, complete with nine bedrooms, ten baths, and lavish decorations by their friend Ronnie Wilson. Cher marveled at the opulence, particularly Chastity's pink-and-white dream bedroom, though her daughter favored the eerie "Dracula's Hideout" tack room.

Despite the grandeur, the house wasn't filled with friends or laughter. Sonny avoided hosting parties except for holidays or Chastity's birthdays, leaving Cher isolated. Her few remaining connections, like Marilyn Wilson, were stifled by Sonny's controlling tendencies. When Marilyn invited her to a Tupperware party, Sonny dismissed it as "dumb," leaving Cher frustrated and lonely.

Then came Paulette, a radiant 21-year-old Armenian woman who crossed Cher's path during a gig in Maryland. Striking and adventurous, Paulette's worldly tales captivated Cher, offering her the companionship she craved. Paulette quickly became Cher's best friend, even earning a nickname, "Cheralina." Sonny underestimated her influence, thinking her young and naïve. But Paulette's vibrant personality and stories of freedom made Cher reflect on her own life.

Back in Los Angeles, Paulette moved to Malibu with Ridgeway, and her presence became a lifeline for Cher. Though Paulette admired Cher's seemingly perfect life, she couldn't see the tension brewing beneath the surface. Cher, struggling with insomnia and weight loss, realized her discontent was growing. "I couldn't eat," she admitted, even during Paulette's birthday celebration. For Cher, the big house and perfect façade weren't enough. Something was missing, and she was beginning to question whether she wanted the life she had so carefully built.

Cher was caught in a whirlwind of conflicting emotions—she loved Sonny, but she wasn't in love with him anymore. Their onstage chemistry was undeniable, but at home, things had unraveled. Sonny, consumed by his dreams of empire-building, barely noticed her feelings. Their once close partnership now felt more like a business arrangement, with Cher toeing the line to avoid conflict.

A LIFE ON THE EDGE

In October 1972, the relentless grind of their career reached its peak. After filming back-to-back shows, they headed to the Sahara's Congo Room in Las Vegas for exhausting two-night performances. Paulette joined Cher in Vegas, bringing much-needed companionship. Paulette helped Cher with simple comforts, but even her presence couldn't mend Cher's growing despair.

One evening, Cher found Sonny immersed in business discussions. She suggested a vacation, only to be dismissed with, "You can't make any money in Europe." Instead, Sonny handed her a contract for another long Vegas stint. Feeling powerless, Cher signed it, suppressing her frustration. She asked Sonny to join her and Paulette at a fair, hoping for a brief escape, but he waved her off. "Just go with Ridgeway and Paulette."

The weight of her isolation became unbearable. Night after night, Cher stood barefoot on the balcony of their suite, staring down at the glittering city below. Each time, thoughts of Chastity, her family, and the people who looked up to her pulled her back. "This can't be the answer," she told herself. Yet the loneliness was suffocating.

One night, as the music drifted up from the hotel below, something clicked. Staring over the edge, she realized that she didn't have to leave; she could leave him.

Cher's unraveling world took an unexpected turn when Paulette shared a seemingly innocent observation: Bill, the young guitarist in their band, had a crush on her. Though flattered, Cher brushed it off. Yet, Paulette's casual mentions of Bill lingered in her mind, like the way he played her riffs during a performance or his quiet attempts to sketch her likeness. Still, Cher hadn't dared to imagine anything more.

After a taxing first show in Vegas, Cher impulsively decided to join Paulette and the band at a nearby Righteous Brothers concert. Tossing on jeans and a T-shirt, she called to Sonny, "I'm going with Pauli and Ridgeway!" His furious reply, "Are you crazy?!" barely registered as she dashed out the door.

At the Hilton Lounge, Cher found herself seated beside Bill. His boldness stunned her when he pulled her close, his hand resting on her knee. For the first time in years, she felt seen. Rushing back for their second show, Sonny berated her, but Cher, calm and defiant, ignored him. Her actions felt reckless but liberating.

Later, Cher joined Paulette in the band's hangout room. When Bill suggested going to the lobby for cigarettes, she followed, despite Paulette's protests. Outside, Cher confessed, "I'm not here for magazines. I wanted to be with you." Stunned, Bill circled her in disbelief, torn between exhilaration and fear.

In the quiet behind the hotel, Bill finally said, "We all wonder how you can live this way." His words pierced her. She hadn't realized others saw her unhappiness. Before she could reply, Bill kissed her, and everything changed. It was the kind of kiss Cher had only dreamed of–a connection she hadn't felt with Sonny in years. For a moment, she remembered what it was like to be cherished.

BREAKING THE CHAINS

Back in Jeff Porcaro's room, Cher sat nervously with the band when the phone rang. Sonny's voice shot through the line: "What do you think you're doing, Cher? What the fuck do you think you're doing?"

"Just hanging with the guys," she replied, her tone steady despite the tension filling the room. Sonny demanded she return to their suite, but Cher, for the first time, pushed back. "Bill wants to talk about his publishing rights," she said, surprising even herself. "I'll bring him up to our suite." Without hesitation, Bill followed her—a boldness that caught her off guard.

Upstairs, Sonny sat in stony silence, watching as the two entered. "Could you go into the bedroom so we can talk?" he asked Bill. Once alone, Sonny, his voice low and trembling, asked, "What do you want to do?"

Cher's answer shocked even her. "I want to sleep with Bill." It wasn't true, but she thought it was the only way to escape. Sonny, caught off guard, asked, "How long do you need?"

"Two hours," she replied, her words cutting through the silence. Sonny left without a word.

In the bedroom, Bill sat quietly, smoking. For the first time, Cher let her guard down, pouring out her unhappiness. "How did it get this way?" he asked, genuinely concerned.

"We were happy once," she said softly. "But he stopped caring. Onstage, it feels like the old days, but offstage, I'm just . . . lost."

They talked into the night until Sonny returned, his presence cold and distant. Without a word, he removed her wedding ring from her finger—a silent end to what had become a loveless marriage.

The next day, Cher found out Sonny had sent Chastity back to LA without consulting her. Furious and drained, she wandered the Strip, trying to process her unraveling world. Later, in a final act of defiance, she asked Sonny for $500 in cash. He handed it over, murmuring, "America will hate you for breaking us up."

Staring him down, Cher replied, "Last night, I didn't care if I was alive or dead."

Later, in Ridgeway's room, Bill begged her, "Come with me, Cher." But she couldn't answer, torn between a life she no longer wanted and the unknown waiting ahead.

A FOGGY ESCAPE AND A NEW BEGINNING

Cher's mind raced when she discovered Sonny had slept with Bill's girlfriend out of revenge. Desperation gripped her, and she blurted to Bill, "Don't go to Texas. Come to San Francisco with me. Sonny gave me money for tickets." Sausalito, the foggy seaside town where she once shared a perfect day with Sonny, felt like a safe haven. To protect her plan, she avoided mentioning Sausalito in front of Pauli and Ridgeway.

When Bill agreed, Cher borrowed sunglasses from Paulette, and Ridgeway reluctantly drove them to the back of the hotel, grumbling, "I'll probably lose my job for this." As Cher cradled Bill's arm, Paulette turned, smiling, "I'm so happy for you!" Ridgeway snapped, "Shut up, Paulette! Do you not understand the ramifications?"

Flying to San Francisco that evening, Cher and Bill took separate cabs, but both got lost in the dense fog. Even Sonny's private detectives couldn't track them. Exhausted, they finally checked into a hotel at 4 a.m. "Where's Sonny?" the clerk asked. Cher hesitated. "Oh, um... he's coming on the next flight."

In their room, Bill kissed her tenderly, and they made love. Cher knew she'd never sleep with Sonny again. Yet, the peace was short-lived. A call from Sonny's associate Denis forced her to return. "It'll be really bad for Bill if you don't come home," Denis warned. For Bill's sake, Cher flew back alone.

At the house, Sonny looked gaunt, sitting at the top of the stairs. Irwin, Sonny's lawyer, laid out the consequences of her decision like it was a business deal, warning her could lose millions if she didn't change course. But Cher was too exhausted to care anymore. In the end, Irwin asked her what she wanted.

Gathering courage, Cher replied, "A place in Malibu and five thousand dollars a month in my own account." Surprisingly, Irwin agreed. The power had shifted. Relieved, Cher collapsed into sleep, only to be awakened later by Sonny, who looked beaten. "What's the matter, bud?" he asked gently. "I want to talk to Bill," she whispered.

Soon after, Bill called. "Let me come to you," he said. Cher promised him a place at her Malibu condo. A week later, she picked him up, wearing a light turquoise suede outfit. They drove to her new home, her freedom solidified.

While Irwin imposed rules to maintain appearances–no public outings with men, limited social activities–Cher didn't care. She was free, with a space of her own and the promise of a fresh start.

CHAPTER 14

BREAKING CHAINS

REDISCOVERING FREEDOM

Just days after leaving Sonny, Cher found herself back onstage with him at CBS. Despite the tension, their chemistry as performers remained intact. "It's good to see you're back," Sonny quipped. Cher, dressed in a revealing gown, shot back, "It's good to see my front too." Sonny glanced at her chest and shrugged, "Same thing." Their banter brought the audience to life. That week, they delivered some of their best performances, particularly a spoof of Chiffon margarine commercials where Cher, as a guru, accidentally improvised, "Go fuck yourself!" instead of her line. Sonny collapsed in hysterics, as did the rest of the crew. Their laughter was genuine, a reminder that despite their personal struggles, their professional partnership was as sharp as ever.

Offstage, Sonny labeled Cher's departure as her "Nagasaki moment" and even gifted her an engraved gold dog tag to mark the event. Media speculation about a fight or abuse at the Sahara Hotel was put to rest by their onstage camaraderie. Their humor and connection weren't an act–Sonny and Cher were still a duo, even if their marriage was over.

Cher began embracing her independence, relishing small freedoms like shopping alone and dressing as she pleased. Life became an adventure, from grocery shopping for the first time in years to discovering simple joys like Ruffles and Dr. Pepper.

Cher also found a new relationship with Bill, a sweet, humorous Texan who cherished her thoughts and made her feel at ease. For the first time, Cher experienced love without restrictions, enjoying moments of tenderness, shared stories, and even the novelty of being asked what she wanted to see at the movies. For Cher, this marked a rebirth–one where she could rediscover herself and finally breathe freely.

Cher's newfound independence was a mix of simple joys and unexpected challenges. Breaking a public agreement with her ex, she ventured to Tower Records with Bill to buy music for her new place. Lost in the aisles, she marveled at the tapes, filling her cart with $600 worth of albums–classics from the Beatles to Stevie Wonder. At home, they stored their growing collection in a chest, revisiting the store whenever new releases dropped. Despite their chemistry, Cher and Bill's time together was limited by her studio work and commitment to being home with Chastity.

One evening, she tried marijuana at Bill's apartment, something she rarely indulged in. Feeling light after one hit, she mistakenly took more when left alone. Soon, she felt dizzy and unsettled, hearing Sonny's voice taunt, "See, I told you something bad would happen if you left me." She sought solace in a bath, overwhelmed by regret.

A SEASON OF TRANSITIONS AND REDISCOVERY

Meanwhile, Cher continued to live in the same house as Sonny to spend time with Chastity. Their vast home allowed space for everyone, including Sonny's assistant Connie, who later became his girlfriend. Cher and Connie developed an unlikely friendship, sharing music-filled moments in Cher's room with Chastity, swearing her to secrecy.

Sonny and Cher's relationship found a new rhythm. Over breakfast, Sonny joked about contemplating throwing Cher off their balcony during a rough patch in their marriage. "I figured I'd plead insanity, write a book, and get my own show," he said. Cher laughed, adding, "I was going to jump anyway!" Their shared humor over past pain showed their evolving bond.

Professionally, Cher embraced her comedic side, debuting "Laverne," a laundromat character adored by fans. With her over-the-top tiger-print jumpsuit, gaudy accessories, and biting humor, Laverne became a hit. Offstage, Cher rekindled her friendship with Joe D, reconnecting him with Chastity, and stood firm in her Democratic beliefs, even removing Nixon signs from her mother's lawn. Cher's journey of freedom, laughter, and self-discovery had only just begun.

That season, Sonny and Cher hosted Ronald Reagan on their show, marking an interesting intersection of entertainment and politics. Sonny presented Reagan with "the coveted Bono award," a humorous Oscar-like statue. Cher couldn't resist adding, "It's even the same size." Reagan was a pleasant guest, but Cher remained skeptical of his presence.

The election party at Jack Benny's home brought a mix of Hollywood's elite, including Lucille Ball, Johnny Carson, and Rosalind Russell. As pundits droned on about vote counts, Lucille cracked irreverent jokes, leaving Cher giggling uncontrollably. Her laughter, however, annoyed Sonny and eventually led to her "banishment" to the den. There, Cher encountered Rosalind Russell, her idol, who offered encouraging words: "You're funny and talented. I think you could be a good actress if you put your mind to it." Rosalind's affirmation joined a mental repository of Cher's inspirations, fueling her belief in her potential.

As Cher and Sonny's relationship evolved into a friendship, moments of their old camaraderie resurfaced. Sonny surprised her one morning by suggesting a weekend trip to Paris. They explored the city, dined, shopped, and even shared playful banter. At the hotel, Cher leaned against the bathtub as Sonny soaked, warning him, "Modern girls won't put up with your controlling ways." Despite her words, Sonny's future relationships followed a familiar pattern: diamonds, Porsches, and the same dynamics.

In January 1973, the *Sonny & Cher Comedy Hour* received a Golden Globe nomination. Cher, dressed in a fox-fur coat over a crop top and skirt, clapped passionately for winners like Liza Minnelli and Diana Ross, imagining her own moment on that stage.

A trip to Hawaii with Paulette brought memories of an earlier visit with Sonny. An elderly couple they'd met reminded Cher of the importance of living fully while young. When Bill arrived in O'ahu, he proposed marriage and a life together in Texas. Cher gently declined, explaining, "I love you, but I'm not divorced, and I have a child." Heartbroken, Bill left, and Cher reflected on her decision, later saying, "I left Sonny for another woman. Me."

SECRETS, SCANDALS, AND STANDING OVATIONS

As the second season of *The Sonny & Cher Comedy Hour* wrapped up in March 1973, Sonny was optimistic about its renewal for a third season. One of the season's standout moments came during their second-to-last episode, when they welcomed Captain John "Spike" Nasmyth, a Vietnam War hero who had endured over six years of captivity under the Vietcong. Gaunt but remarkably composed, Spike shared how Sonny and Cher's music had uplifted him and his fellow prisoners in the infamous "Hanoi Hilton." The audience erupted in a standing ovation. Deeply moved, Sonny and Cher gifted him all their albums recorded during his captivity.

At the time, both wore POW/MIA bracelets as a tribute to prisoners of war. Cher's bracelet bore the name of Second Lieutenant Hayden Lockhart Jr., who later appeared on the show to receive it from her in person. Cher described him as a young, sweet man whose name would forever remain in her heart.

Amid their professional highs, Cher and Sonny celebrated Chas's fourth birthday with a garden party filled with pony rides, balloons, and a clown. Cher invited Joe D, marking the first time he and Sonny were in the same space since their falling out. Thankfully, tensions stayed at bay, and the children were enthralled by guest Carol Burnett, whom they regarded as a bigger star than Sonny and Cher.

That spring, Cher's golden outfit stole the show as she and Sonny presented an award at the 45th Academy Awards. Beneath the glitz, Cher struggled with deep emotional turmoil. Sonny suggested therapy, but Cher later discovered her therapist was secretly reporting her sessions back to Sonny. Feeling betrayed, Cher confronted him. "How could you do this?" she screamed, but Sonny had no defense.

The betrayals ran deeper. Joe D revealed Sonny's years of infidelity, detailing secret trysts during their tours. Cher was stunned, not just by his actions, but by how oblivious she had been. As others began confessing to her, she realized the extent of Sonny's lies, each revelation cutting deeper. "You must have known," they told her, but Cher hadn't.

THE TOUR THAT TESTED EVERYTHING

In May 1973, Cher recorded *Half-Breed*, her second solo album produced by Snuff Garrett, and its title track would later become her second solo number-one hit. After completing the album, she and Sonny embarked on a grueling summer tour, performing one-night gigs across the country. Paulette and Ridgeway were part of the crew, and Cher cherished having her friend with her. During the tour, Cher grew closer to David Paich, their pianist, who brought her moments of lighthearted connection. Their friendship briefly turned physical before settling back into a platonic bond.

One night in Iowa, after a successful performance, Cher, Paulette, and members of the band gathered on the playground behind their motel. It was an innocent moment of camaraderie–swinging, laughing, and chatting in the open air. Cher felt content, but things took a sinister turn. Paulette rushed to Cher's room later, saying that Sonny's right-hand man, Denis, had threatened the band members. Denis warned David that his fingers might be broken and Jeffrey that his Porsche could be blown up. Sonny's old-school Sicilian protectiveness wasn't charming this time; it was terrifying.

By the next day, the band had turned cold. Under threat of being fired, they stopped talking to Cher entirely. Even Paulette, Cher's best friend, distanced herself, citing fear of losing her job. Cher was heartbroken and felt utterly alone. "Cher, what do you want me to do? Everyone's scared of Sonny," Paulette pleaded. Cher, seething with betrayal, couldn't hide her anger, even on stage. During a performance, she turned her back on Sonny for the entirety of *I Got You Babe*. The team criticized her as unprofessional, but Cher couldn't pretend everything was fine.

Returning home, Cher reunited with Chas, finding solace in her daughter's love. Back at CBS for the third season of *The Sonny & Cher Comedy Hour*, Sonny returned to his jovial self. Yet, Cher remained uneasy, unsure of what had provoked his fury.

During a live album recording in Vegas, Sonny's wistful words about their early days hit Cher hard. He spoke of their humble beginnings, their old brass bed, and their philosophy of enduring life's challenges together. While his nostalgic tone seemed genuine, Cher couldn't reconcile the man he was with the man he had become. She still loved parts of him but realized she could never fully understand him anymore.

CHAPTER 15

FROM LOVE TO LAWSUITS

THE BEGINNING OF SOMETHING SPECIAL

In December 1973, Cher decided to attend Lou Adler's Christmas party despite Sonny's objections. "No, you're not going," Sonny insisted. Cher, unyielding, replied, "Yeah, and you can come with me or stay home, but I'm going." They arrived together, though Cher quickly found herself on the floor, laughing with Goldie Hawn, who was lounging in a onesie. The party buzzed with energy, but Cher and Goldie were lost in their own conversation until a man walked in. "David! Come sit with us," Goldie called out.

Cher recognized him from the Troubadour but assumed he was a promotion guy for Ahmet Ertegun. David Geffen joined them, and Cher found him captivating. Two days later, David called, inviting her to dinner. Intrigued, Cher agreed.

Driving to his Spanish-style home on Copley Drive, just blocks from her own, Cher was surprised. "How does a promotion man afford a house like this?" she wondered. David greeted her in jeans and a plaid shirt, phone cord trailing behind him, and ushered her in. Dinner was unexpected–Lou Adler joined them. Though surprised, Cher enjoyed the meal, including her first taste of avocado soup.

After dinner, Lou left, and David and Cher talked all night. Sharing their stories, she realized David wasn't just anyone; he was a powerhouse in the music industry, managing icons like Joni Mitchell and the Eagles.

By morning, Cher felt like she'd known David forever. He was kind, shy, and incredibly smart. David didn't want her to leave, but Cher had to be at CBS in hours. He invited her to Robbie Robertson's house the next night, and she agreed.

The following evening, David confessed, "I told my psychiatrist I think I'm in love with you." Cher panicked, scooting away in her seat. "Oh fuck," she thought. At Robbie's candlelit dinner, surrounded by warmth and conversation, Cher began to see David differently. "There's something special about him," she realized.

Their connection deepened over time. They spent more evenings together, slipping into a relationship. For David, it was his first love. For Cher, it was something new, something extraordinary. "Maybe I have to rethink this," she mused. Soon, they were inseparable, quietly building something beautiful away from the public eye.

David was an early riser, his routine vastly different from Cher's late-night habits. She often stayed until he fell asleep, slipping out just as Joni Mitchell returned from the studio. Occasionally, Joni would share her demos, and one night she said, "Cher, you have this beautiful green light around you, like a gentle aura." Cher smiled, touched by the compliment. During this time, Joni was working on *Court and Spark*, an album that would become a huge hit, with one song, "Free Man in Paris," written about David Geffen.

David, known for his calm demeanor with Cher, revealed a fiery side in business. She often overheard his intense arguments with entertainment lawyer David Braun. "He never lost," she noted, amazed by his ability to balance tenderness with ruthless determination.

Meanwhile, Sonny began to notice Cher's frequent visits to David and grew uneasy. Everyone in the industry knew David Geffen, and Sonny's insecurities began to show. Their once-lighthearted dynamic at work soured, and Sonny's goofy charm on their show faded.

David, on the other hand, was a deeply loving boyfriend. One evening, their friend Tony Fantozzi joined them for dinner at David's. Tony, once close to Sonny, shocked Cher by suggesting, "How does *The Cher Show* sound to you?" Outraged by the disloyalty, Cher's anger flared. "Does anyone have values anymore?" she thought. David, equally livid, asked Tony to leave. It was a betrayal Cher couldn't forgive.

On Valentine's Day, Cher ran errands, unaware of the date. Returning to her car, she found a gift bag tied to the steering wheel. Inside was a Cartier diamond bracelet and a heartfelt note from David. Cher was overwhelmed–Sonny had never celebrated Valentine's Day with her. Though Sonny had given expensive jewelry, it had always felt performative, not personal. David's thoughtfulness, however, moved her deeply.

THE FINAL STRAW

As their relationship grew, David grew curious about Cher's contracts. When he finally read them, he was horrified. "Sweetheart, this contract is involuntary servitude," he told her. Cher, stunned, learned that she had no rights, no money, and no control over her career. "You're an employee of Cher Enterprises," David explained, revealing that Sonny owned ninety-five percent, with the remaining five percent belonging to his lawyer, Irwin Spiegel. Cher had unknowingly signed away everything.

Heartbroken, Cher sat in disbelief. "I don't own one of the houses?

What am I going to do?" she asked. David reassured her, "We'll get you out of this." With David by her side, Cher found the strength to face the betrayal, though the full horror of Sonny's actions took days to sink in. The man she had trusted most had orchestrated her downfall, leaving her to rebuild from the ground up.

Cher couldn't stop wondering what had gone through Sonny's mind when he and Irwin drew up the contract. "Did they celebrate after, light cigars, and laugh?" she thought bitterly. She suspected it all stemmed from her rebellion after returning from Sausalito. "What can you do if someone stops caring?" she mused. Sonny had always been instrumental in their success, but Cher now realized he wouldn't have gotten far without her voice and comedic talent. Yet something darker within Sonny had surfaced–a side she couldn't reconcile with the man she once loved.

Confused and betrayed, Cher called Lucille Ball for advice. "Lucy, I want to leave Sonny. What should I do?" she asked, knowing Lucy had faced a similar situation with Desi Arnaz. "Fuck him," Lucy replied bluntly. "You're the one with the talent." It was exactly what Cher needed to hear.

David Geffen urged her to get a lawyer, dismissing her reliance on Irwin. "He's Sonny's lawyer," David said. "You need your own." David arranged for Cher to meet Mickey Rudin, a top attorney who had represented Frank Sinatra and helped Lucy extricate herself from Desi. Mickey told her the first step was filing for divorce.

Despite her anger, Cher felt compelled to confront Sonny in person. She met him in his office, lit a cigarette, and stared him down. "Son, I've had someone look over my contract. It says I'm your employee. That can't be right. I'm your partner. Your wife. We built this together."

Sonny, lighting a cigar, remained cold. "I want my half, Sonny," Cher demanded. "You need to tear up that contract and make me a 50-50 partner."

But Sonny refused. "I'm not going to do that," he said emotionlessly. Cher was stunned. "If you don't, I won't sign for another year with CBS," she warned. "I can't keep working for nothing."

"You'll get sued," Sonny countered.

"I don't care."

Sonny shrugged, confident she wouldn't follow through. His once-jovial demeanor had vanished, replaced by a chilling indifference. Cher realized the man she had loved and trusted was gone, replaced by someone she barely recognized.

Determined, Cher called Fred Silverman, head of CBS programming. "Freddie, it's me. I need you to not pick up the show," she pleaded. She explained her situation, promising she wouldn't defect to another network. Though surprised, Fred listened, sensing her desperation.

Sonny had built their empire on her talent, and now Cher was ready to fight for what was hers—even if it meant tearing it all down.

THE CURTAIN FALLS

Cher's return to CBS for *The Sonny & Cher Comedy Hour* was marked by a mix of nerves and nostalgia. On her first day back, she unexpectedly ran into Sonny in the corridor, where their mutual awkwardness quickly dissolved into laughter. Despite their personal struggles, the pair delivered seamless performances, even singing "Will You Love Me Tomorrow" arm in arm, as if nothing had changed. However, Sonny's formal "Thank you very much, bud" after each show hinted at the strain beneath the surface.

Behind the scenes, things were unraveling. Rumors spread that Cher was negotiating a deal with NBC for her own show, forcing her to reassure CBS executives of her loyalty. Despite her efforts, CBS canceled *The Sonny & Cher Comedy Hour* in March 1974, ending its fourth season before it began. Cher had sacrificed the show to save herself, a decision that left Sonny and their collaborators furious.

The fallout was brutal. Sonny demanded that Cher move out of their dream house, claiming it was for "publicity reasons." With nowhere else to go, she stayed briefly with David, who supported her during this tumultuous time. He rented her a house in Malibu, where she found solace surrounded by friends and family. The new home provided a much-needed refuge as Cher began rebuilding her life.

On January 21, 1974, Sonny and Cher recorded their final show together, drawing a crowd of emotional fans who had lined up for hours to witness the bittersweet moment. Producer Chris Bearde acknowledged the audience's sadness, urging them to appreciate the love that still existed between Sonny and Cher. The duo's final duet was deeply moving, and Cher's solo performance of Stevie Wonder's "All in Love Is Fair" left no dry eye in the studio.

Just days later, Cher was stunned to win a Golden Globe for Best Actress in a Musical or Comedy Television Series. Ironically, she had skipped the ceremony, convinced Carol Burnett would win. Hearing her name announced while having her nails done, Cher was overwhelmed by the unexpected recognition during such a challenging time in her life. The award was a glimmer of hope as she prepared to move forward from one of the most emotional chapters of her career.

Days later, at the Golden Globes, Cher skipped the ceremony, certain she wouldn't win over the legendary Carol Burnett. As her nails were being done, she heard the announcer call her name for Best Actress.

For David's February birthday, Cher helped organize a surprise party at the Beverly Wilshire Hotel's Grand Trianon room. The carnival-themed celebration featured knife throwers, unicyclists, fire eaters, mimes, and even a fortune teller. A-list guests filled the room, including Warren Beatty, Jack Nicholson, and Ringo Starr. When Mo Ostin brought David in, the crowd erupted in applause. Cher sang "Happy Birthday," followed by a set with Bob Dylan harmonizing on "All I Really Want to Do" and Rick Danko joining her for "Mockingbird." Dylan closed the night with "Mr. Tambourine Man," making it unforgettable.

Days later, on February 18, Sonny shocked Cher by filing for divorce. The media exploded with sensational headlines about "the Battling Bonos." Despite the chaos, the duo flew to Houston to perform at the Livestock Show and Rodeo alongside Elvis and the Jackson 5. Cher's makeshift dressing room was a disaster–a wooden booth in the arena. Mid-costume change, her hair caught in her jumpsuit zipper. Laughing hysterically, she was trapped until Sonny cut her free with scissors. The show went on, even with her jumpsuit barely held together.

Back in Los Angeles, Mickey Rudin filed Cher's divorce papers, accusing Sonny of holding her in "involuntary servitude" and violating the Constitution. Sonny retaliated with lawsuits against both Cher and David, claiming millions in losses and accusing David of interference. Cher and Sonny, despite the legal battles, stayed civil when discussing Chas.

On March 2, Cher and David attended the Grammys together, marking their public debut as a couple. The press dubbed them "the industry's hottest couple," though the attention visibly unnerved David. Cher held his hand throughout the night, guiding him through the frenzy.

HARMONY, CHAOS, AND HEARTBREAK

A month later, Cher presented the Academy Award for Best Original

Dramatic Score to Marvin Hamlisch for *The Way We Were*. Nervously, she butchered his name but laughed it off. Backstage, a brief encounter with Katharine Hepburn left Cher starstruck. "She spoke to me!" Cher thought, cherishing the moment.

Despite the whirlwind, Cher focused on her music, finishing her *Dark Lady* album. Its title track soared to number one, cementing her place in the industry. Surrounded by icons like Jack Nicholson, Joni Mitchell, and the Eagles, Cher felt inspired to elevate her artistry, determined to thrive amid the chaos.

David's suggestion to collaborate with big names like Jimmy Webb or Phillip Spector led Cher to A&M Studios after finishing her album with Snuffy. Phillip was producing John Lennon's *Rock 'n' Roll* album and invited Cher and Harry Nilsson to record background vocals. Arriving at the studio, they found John storming out, shouting, "I'm never gonna work with that madman again. He's fucking nuts!" A chair crashed behind him. Phillip, unbothered, asked Cher and Harry to lay down a guide vocal for "A Love Like Yours." Weeks later, she discovered Phillip had released the track illegally, breaching their contracts.

Furious, Cher confronted Phillip at his eerie, mansion-like home. As he dismissed her complaints and twirled a revolver on his fingers, Cher snapped. "Don't fuck with me, Phillip! Put that gun down and promise me this won't happen again." Shaken, she left, but the incident haunted her.

Later, Cher ran into John Lennon and Harry Nilsson at a bar. Harry begged her to take them to Hugh Hefner's Sunday movie night. The casual gathering turned chaotic as the drunk duo disrupted the event with chants of "Huff! Huff! Huff!" Mortified, Cher ushered them outside, only to find them naked in the Grotto. Laughing despite herself, she herded them back into their clothes, feeling like a babysitter to two rowdy teens.

Amid the chaos, Cher's divorce proceedings loomed large. Her lawyers negotiated the division of $28 million in assets, a staggering sum for the time. David tirelessly supported her, ensuring she was protected. In March 1974, David arranged for Cher and her sister, Gee, to visit their ailing father, John Southall, in Texas. Seeing him frail and yellowed from liver failure broke Cher's heart. His joy at their visit was evident, and though Cher wanted to say more, she stayed quiet, prioritizing Gee's emotions. He passed away days later, but Cher was grateful for their final moments together.

Cher's beach house in Malibu became a haven. Chas initially adored David, and the three of them often played together. One memorable evening, she ran into the bathroom while David was in the tub, chatting away and splashing the water until Cher gently moved her back. But Chas's feelings shifted, mirroring Sonny's attitude toward David, which upset both Cher and David. Recognizing how it affected Chas, Cher and Sonny made a pact never to speak negatively about each other or their partners around her, a promise they honored and were proud to uphold.

CHAPTER 16

FROM COURTROOMS TO CATWALKS

COURTROOM BATTLES AND A HOMECOMING

And then Sonny devastated Cher by seeking full custody of Chas during their divorce, accusing her of being an unfit mother. His case focused on an innocent visit to Hugh Hefner's home, where Cher had taken Chas to see the pet monkeys and swim in the pool. To Chas, the house was a magical place where she could enjoy ice cream served by a waiter in the Grotto. Sonny's lawyer, Irwin Spiegel, twisted the visit into something sordid, calling it a trip to a "house of fornication." Cher was filled with anxiety at the thought of losing custody or only seeing Chas on weekends. Despite Sonny's bond with their daughter, Cher couldn't fathom why he'd try to take her away.

In May, Cher and Sonny appeared in the Santa Monica courthouse to address the latest developments in their divorce. With Paulette by her side, Cher watched as Mickey Rudin methodically dismantled Sonny's accusations. The judge, previously critical of Cher for breaking her contract, now warned Irwin Spiegel to tread carefully or risk a defamation lawsuit. Though the judge seemed sympathetic to Cher regarding custody, he postponed his final decision, leaving everyone in suspense.

As they exited the courthouse, reporters swarmed, shouting questions. Cher stood silently as Sonny prepared to respond. Suddenly, he grabbed her face, kissed her dramatically, and burst into laughter as cameras flashed. Stunned, Cher couldn't help but laugh too, despite wanting to be angry. Sonny's absurd sense of humor had struck again, even amidst the chaos.

Ultimately, the judge ruled in Cher's favor, granting her primary custody of Chas and reducing Sonny's visitation time. Shocked, Sonny asked, "Are you really going to stick to that?" Cher rolled her eyes and replied, "Of course not, dummy. You can see her whenever you like." She never intended to keep Chas from him.

Meanwhile, the financial negotiations dragged on, and Cher missed her beloved big house. At David's suggestion, Mickey Rudin advised her to simply move back in. Nervous but determined, Cher and David returned one morning while Sonny was out. Connie, now a friend, called Sonny to inform him, but to Cher's relief, he did nothing. Days later, Sonny had his belongings moved to the St. Cloud house, which Cher had signed over to him.

Cher was thrilled to reclaim her dream home and welcomed David, who moved in with his German butler Klaus and cook Ida. Delighted, Cher looked forward to hosting the elegant dinners she'd always dreamed of, with Ida's famous chilled avocado soup on the menu. Finally, she felt a sense of peace returning to her life.

TRAGEDY, UNCERTAINTY, AND NEW BEGINNINGS

In July 1974, Cher's joy was shattered by the news of Cass Elliot's sudden death at just thirty-two. After performing at the London Palladium, Cass had attended Mick Jagger's birthday party and spent the evening socializing before retiring to Harry Nilsson's apartment. That night, she passed away from a heart attack. On the day of her funeral, Michelle Phillips arrived at Cher's door with Cass's seven-year-old daughter, Owen. The little girl looked up at Cher and said, "My mom's dead." Cher embraced her, comforting her as Chas kept her company.

At Mount Sinai Cemetery, Cher joined a crowd of luminaries, including Carol Burnett and Robert Redford, to honor Cass. Cher couldn't help but recall Cass's humor and reckless charm, like when she sped down Mulholland Drive in her Mini Cooper, laughing as Cher begged her to slow down.

In July 1974, Cher attended a Troubadour gig featuring the Average White Band. Afterward, she accompanied the band to a party in the Hollywood Hills, deciding to go alone for the first time. The host, Ken Moss, offered drugs, but Cher declined. The night took a dark turn when band members Alan Gorrie and Robbie McIntosh fell ill after taking a drug Moss provided.

Cher quickly stepped into crisis mode. While Alan was nauseous and weak, Robbie was unconscious in a bathtub with blue fingernails–a clear sign of oxygen deprivation. Panicked, Cher called a doctor, who urged her to get Robbie to a hospital immediately. Despite her pleas, Moss dismissed her concerns, claiming Robbie would recover by morning.

Cher took Alan to her home, cared for him through the night, and helped him recover. Tragically, the next day brought devastating news: Robbie had died. The drug, a lethal mix of heroin and morphine, had claimed the life of the 24-year-old drummer, leaving behind a wife and child.

David returned to find Cher inconsolable and insisted on contacting the police. Cher became a key witness in the case, her testimony leading to Moss's conviction for involuntary manslaughter. However, the press spun lurid stories about Cher's involvement, painting the night as a seedy drug-fueled scandal.

The accusations stung deeply, with headlines questioning her character and motherhood. "All I did was try to save a life," Cher lamented. Despite the chaos, she stood firm, knowing she had done what she could. The night left her shaken but resolute—determined to face the scrutiny with the strength she'd always summoned in moments of crisis.

CHER'S UNFORGETTABLE YEAR

Amid her grief, Cher learned that Sonny had signed with ABC for *The Sonny Comedy Revue*. The show, a near replica of *The Sonny & Cher Comedy Hour*, featured celebrity guests like Glen Campbell and the Jackson 5. Sonny's quip that "there wouldn't be an Indian standing there" when he looked left stung. Cher didn't want him to fail but feared her own future if he succeeded. Living in a house she couldn't afford, she wondered what lay ahead.

Sensing her unease, David Geffen negotiated a deal with CBS for Cher's solo show, simply titled *Cher*. Thrilled but nervous, Cher worked with designer Bob Mackie to create a bold, single-woman image. "I don't want to look like a housewife in an evening gown," she told him. Bob laughed, "Oh, Cher, my dear, we'll never worry about that!"

As Sonny's show struggled against tough competition, CBS announced *Cher* would air Sundays at 8 p.m., directly competing with Sonny's. The rivalry never materialized—Sonny's show was canceled before hers began. David's unwavering support had carried Cher through loss, uncertainty, and into the next chapter of her career.

In November 1974, Cher was invited to the Met Gala, which Diana Vreeland had transformed into a high-fashion, celebrity-filled extravaganza at the Metropolitan Museum of Art. The theme, "Romantic and Glamorous Hollywood Design," felt tailor-made for Cher. She asked Bob Mackie to escort her and create the perfect outfit. Her choice? The now-iconic "souffle dress," a daring gown of beads and feathers that clung to her skin like magic when sprayed with water. Crafted from highly flammable material smuggled in from France, the dress made her look nearly naked, a fact that sparked controversy and fascination alike.

At the gala, her daring look stole the spotlight. A guest even asked, "How does it feel to be naked?" Cher laughed, replying, "It feels great." Richard Avedon's photo of her in "the naked dress" later graced the cover of *Time* in March 1975, causing a sensation. Though it sold out, the issue was banned in parts of the South for its audacity. Cher, however, reveled in the attention, calling the dress simply "the dress" from then on.

The Met Gala itself was a star-studded affair. Cher mingled with legends like Liza Minnelli, Andy Warhol, and Jackie Kennedy. Some of her own costumes, designed by Bob Mackie, were included in the evening's exhibit, elevating her from TV star to a symbol of high fashion. While in New York, she sat for Andy Warhol's *Interview* magazine, styled spectacularly by Ara Gallant with Christmas lights woven into her braids.

Back in Los Angeles, David threw a grand Christmas party at their Carolwood house. Paulette and Gee compiled a guest list brimming with every hot musician and heartthrob they could think of. The night was a massive success, though Paulette spent much of it begrudgingly giving house tours on David's insistence. David surprised Cher with a diamond necklace, though it turned out smaller than expected due to misleading ads. Still, the gesture touched her.

The Met Gala, "the dress," and the party cemented Cher's status as both a cultural and fashion icon, marking 1974 as a turning point in her life and career.

HOTELS, AND HASH DENS

Cher, Paulette, and Gee arrived in Paris for their holiday with an absurd twenty-two suitcases, jet-lagged and starving, Paulette, the only one fluent in French–albeit with a hilariously awful accent–handled room service at the luxurious Hôtel de Crillon. After dinner, Cher took over as their makeup artist, a ritual she found meditative. It took them hours to get ready, but they felt glamorous in their designer coats and Bob Mackie cape.

As they strolled through the hotel lobby, two Frenchwomen argued nearby. One approached Cher and exclaimed, "That woman thought you were hookers, but I told her, 'Non, non, non, that is Cher, a famous American TV star!' Je m'excuse." Amused, Cher shared the story with Paulette and Gee, and they laughed hysterically.

After a few extravagant nights, they moved to the Hôtel Raphael, a more affordable option. Their Parisian adventures led them to the hottest dance spots, where they jokingly told everyone they were searching for Johnny Rivers. At Dani's, they marveled at Jerry Hall's audacious presence in a fishnet catsuit. Paulette drew her own attention, catching the eye of writer-director Pierre Billon, who once rode a motorcycle into a restaurant to find her.

From Paris, they headed to Amsterdam, booking a budget "boutique" hotel atop a five-story walk-up. Exhausted from lugging Louis Vuitton suitcases–dubbed "hooker luggage" by a Parisian waiter–they ventured into a nightclub. The place reeked of hash, which Cher only realized after seeing three people arrested for heroin. When a man mistook her mints for LSD, she knew it was time to leave.

Outside, stranded without a cab, they hitched a ride with stoned American boys in a Volkswagen van. One slurred, "Can't you just make a sacrifuck?" cracking them all up. Even in chaos, the trio created unforgettable memories.

Back in Paris, Paulette met Johnny Hallyday, France's rock-and-roll icon, leaving Pierre in the past. The trio then flew to London, checking into a doll-sized hotel where the tiny elevator and ninety-seven-year-old baggage man made moving their excessive luggage a 40-minute ordeal. Cramped and unimpressed, they attempted to find better accommodations. After numerous rejections, Cher called Joe D, who pulled strings with Hugh Hefner to secure a suite at the Playboy Club.

Excited, they arrived only to find the suite littered with old chicken boxes and pizza. Exhausted, they sat on their mountain of luggage until Joe D redirected them to a house owned by Hef's friend, Bernie Cornfeld. Upon arriving, a mix-up led them to wake up a woman in bunny slippers before finding Bernie's home. Bernie, clad in a tiny kimono that revealed more than they wished to see, welcomed them. Cher's awkward encounter with Bernie in her room, armed with only hand towels, culminated in all three women sharing a bed to escape the musty basement Bernie had assigned Paulette and Gee.

The next morning, they left for a normal hotel, finally finding peace in a hot bath and a quiet evening watching a documentary.

Back in Los Angeles, David, who had missed Cher, whisked her off to Aspen with friends like Jack Nicholson and Anjelica Huston. Cher was enchanted by Aspen's energy, independent shops, and relaxed atmosphere. She embraced skiing and danced all night, feeling free from Hollywood pressures.

Amid their trip, David proposed marriage again, and Cher agreed but requested they wait until winter, hoping to marry in Aspen after her divorce was finalized. Their love grew stronger as they returned to Los Angeles, with David planning their future, while Cher adjusted to the idea of a new chapter in her life.

CHAPTER 17

THE SPOTLIGHT RECLAIMED

SOLO DEBUT

On January 6, 1975, Cher stepped onto the stage alone for the premiere of her new show. Surrounded by her trusted team–Art Fisher directing, Bob Mackie designing costumes, and Paulette, Gee, and her mother backstage–she still felt petrified. The absence of Sonny left a void; there was no one to turn to and ask, "How am I doing, Son?" Standing in darkness, the first piano notes of "Let Me Entertain You" began. Nervous but determined, Cher sang under a solo spotlight. Then, with a dramatic flourish, she revealed a nude tulle rhinestone dress that drew audible gasps from the audience. As she strutted down a moving runway, she teased, "Can I hear a little commotion for the dress? Okay, now let's hear it for the back of the dress."

Cher's opening monologue was a mix of vulnerability and charm. Staring into the camera, she introduced herself: "My name is Cher. I am twenty-eight years old, five feet seven and a half inches tall...and my fate is in your hands." With that, the show began, featuring an incredible lineup of guests: Elton John, Flip Wilson, and Bette Midler. Elton joined her for "Lucy in the Sky with Diamonds," followed by Flip and Bette in sketches that showcased their comedic chemistry. One standout segment, "The Final Curtain," saw the trio hilariously playing aged retirees reminiscing about their showbiz days in 2025, with Bob Mackie's whimsical costumes stealing the scene.

For the finale, Cher, Elton, and Bette performed a medley of hits, dazzling in silver-and-white costumes on a dreamy set filled with balloons. The premiere was a resounding success, drawing 21 million viewers and outperforming *The Wonderful World of Disney*–a feat no other show had achieved. Cher was overwhelmed with gratitude, acknowledging David's pivotal role in getting her career back on track.

However, life as a single woman in the spotlight came with challenges. The censors, seemingly oblivious during *The Sonny & Cher Show*, now scrutinized every detail of her wardrobe and performances. Bob Mackie often clashed with them, and Cher herself sought help from Norman Lear when a beautiful solo was deemed "too suggestive." Despite the obstacles, Cher's wit and resilience carried her through, cementing her place as a solo star.

A FIERY ROMANCE

Before Gregg Allman started playing that night, the room was noisy with chatter and movement. As the lights dimmed, a figure quietly made his way to the piano. He began to play, and within seconds, the room fell silent. When the lights came up, Gregg's presence was mesmerizing—his long blond hair, deep blue eyes, and calm demeanor radiated a quiet intensity. The crowd hung on every note as if hypnotized.

After his set, the room darkened again while the stage crew reset for Etta James. During the lull, Gregg's right-hand man, Chank, handed Cher a note. Curious but casual, she pocketed it, brushing off her sister Gee's insistence to read it. Finally, under the light of a cigarette machine, Cher unfolded the note and smiled at its flowery tone. Gregg addressed her as "Dear enchanting lady" and invited her to return the next night, promising to play for her. He left his phone number and signed it "Gregg Allman." Intrigued but not immediately swooning, Cher pocketed the note, deciding days later to call him and suggest dinner instead.

When the night came, Cher agonized over what to wear. Her assistant Pauli confidently predicted Gregg would arrive in a hand-tooled North Beach leather ensemble. True to her guess, Gregg showed up dressed as if out of a rock-and-roll catalog. Nervously fidgeting, he handed Cher a gift—a small wooden box adorned with an enamel moon and stars. Inside was a tiny pink stone elephant, a thoughtful token she still treasures.

But the date itself was a disaster. Gregg first took her to Dino's, a dimly lit restaurant where their conversation floundered. Trying to impress, he offered to fly her to Hawaii for the weekend. Cher, unimpressed, shot back, "Does that work on other girls?" The night only got worse at a chaotic party at the Continental Hyatt. Surrounded by drugged-out guests, Cher felt completely out of place. When Gregg tried to kiss her, she pulled away, exclaiming, "Whoa, dude, why don't you just take me home?" As she left his car, Gregg delivered a snarky farewell: "Tell your secretary I said hello."

In all, the night was a massive disappointment.

The next day Cher found herself at CBS, sobbing while being fitted for costumes. Dating felt foreign to her; she'd never dated Sonny, and her relationship with David had started with a simple dinner. "Last night was terrible. I'll never be good at this," she confessed to Paulette.

When Gregg called the next day, she didn't hold back. "That was the worst date I ever had," she told him. Gregg agreed, admitting,

"Me too. Can we try again?" Amused, Cher laughed and eventually agreed. Their second date was entirely different. At the Candy Store nightclub, they danced until they were drenched in sweat. Later, sitting and talking, Gregg let his guard down, no longer trying to impress her. Over the next few days, they became inseparable until Gregg returned to Macon and resumed touring. Despite the distance, they talked constantly, their connection growing deeper.

As news of their relationship spread, tabloids speculated about Cher's new love. *Esquire* ran a cover story asking, "Who's man enough for this woman?" Cher laughed at the irony, given that some publications had previously linked her to Elvis and Robert Redford–two men she'd never even met. David, however, wasn't amused. Hurt, he told Cher, "If we're walking on the street and I'm on one side, cross to the other." It was painful for her, as she still cared deeply for him.

When Gregg returned during a tour break, their love intensified. Despite his "bad boy" image, he was soft-spoken and kind, with a Southern charm that reminded her of her grandparents. Cher affectionately called him "Gui Gui," and he nicknamed her "Chooch," meaning "eloquently funky." Their nights together often ended with Gregg serenading her in bed, his voice as beautiful as his glowing, rosy-cheeked face.

Their romance wasn't without excitement. One night, after falling asleep with a candle lit, Cher awoke to find the bedroom on fire. Gregg acted fast, extinguishing the flames with wet towels. By the next day, Cher had completely redecorated the room in a modern Balinese style.

A SOULFUL CONNECTION AND A PAINFUL TRUTH

Despite warnings about Gregory's drug use, Cher didn't want to listen. He seemed kind, sweet, and easy to be around, rarely drinking. Though his habit of wearing long-sleeve shirts, even to bed, raised questions, Gregory's excuse that he sweated too much seemed plausible. Cher dismissed concerns about heroin, convinced by the flawed logic that heroin addicts didn't engage in intimacy.

During a weekend trip to Gregory's home in Macon, Cher experienced his world. She met two kind women, Inez Hill and Louise Hudson, renowned for their soul food, and Chank Middleton, Gregory's loyal best friend who referred to her as "Ms. Allman." Chank's warmth contrasted with the band members, some of whom undermined Gregory's confidence. Dickey Betts, however, welcomed her and proudly spoke of the band's support for their Democratic governor,

Jimmy Carter, whose values on civil rights resonated with them.

Eventually, Gregory introduced Cher to his mother, Alice, or "Mama A." Her tragic past revealed the roots of Gregory's pain. Willis, Gregory's father, had been murdered when Gregory was two, and his brother, Duane, was killed in a motorcycle accident years later. When Mama A shared her scrapbook, it abruptly ended at Duane's death. Her candid remark, "There was no reason to keep a scrapbook after Duane died," visibly hurt Gregory.

Driving through Macon in Gregory's Corvette, Cher learned more about his struggles. Duane had convinced Gregory to join the Allman Brothers, pulling him away from dental school. Duane, a surrogate father figure, had been Gregory's anchor until his untimely death.

Their connection deepened as Gregory opened up about his pain. Early one morning, he confessed, "I'm a heroin addict, Chooch." Stunned, Cher didn't know how to respond but saw his admission as a breakthrough. When she shared this with her mother, she was met with a simple yet profound question: "Do you love him?" Through tears, Cher replied, "Yes." Her mother's advice was clear: "Then bring him home."

A VEGAS WEDDING

Determined to help Gregory Allman overcome his heroin addiction, Cher and her friend Paulette took turns caring for him around the clock, sacrificing sleep and energy. After a grueling ten days, Gregory was sober, but Cher's decision to stand by him came with immense scrutiny. Rumors swirled, fueled by her association with a rock star, and many questioned her commitment to someone with such struggles. Cher, however, saw Gregory's kind, sweet nature when he was sober and believed in his ability to change.

Despite their love, blending Gregory's rock-and-roll life with Cher's world wasn't easy. Cher fought to include him on her show, but the appearance backfired. His fans disapproved, hers weren't receptive, and the experiment left both feeling misplaced. Cher still supported Gregory at his performances, even enduring the brazenness of his fans. Once, while a girl handed him her number, Gregory exclaimed, "I'm talking to my wife!"–a term he used to assert her importance, even before they married.

In March 1975, Cher and Gregory attended a star-studded party hosted by Paul McCartney on the Queen Mary. They mingled with legends like George Harrison and Bob Dylan, and Cher danced with Michael

Jackson. Later that year, Joe D organized Cher's lavish twenty-ninth birthday at PIPS, a celebrity hotspot, where even Sonny showed up with a new girlfriend. Despite the celebrations, Cher's life remained in flux.

By late June, her long, complicated divorce from Sonny was finalized. Days later, Cher discovered she was pregnant with Gregory's child. They decided to marry. With Paulette and Gee in tow, they flew to Las Vegas on a private jet arranged by Joe D. Dressed in a simple powder-blue outfit, Cher walked into a suite at Caesars Palace, where Judge James Brennan officiated the intimate ceremony. Though smiling for the cameras, Cher wrestled with doubts. "What is your plan, Cher?" she wondered. Yet, she pushed forward, knowing the future was unwritten.

Cher and Gregory Allman's marriage began on shaky ground. The day after their wedding, Gregory was gone, and Cher discovered a bag of white powder in his forgotten Dopp kit. Exhausted and uncertain, she lacked the strength to confront him. As their fragile bond faltered, Cher focused on her pregnancy, but complications led her doctor to suggest a decision. With no support from Gregory, she chose to terminate the pregnancy, trusting her doctor's care.

The strain of their relationship deepened when Cher learned from a press agent–and later confirmed by Gregory's friend Dickey Betts–that Gregory had filed for divorce. Though he denied it initially, the truth emerged, prompting Cher to file her own papers just nine days after their wedding. The media frenzy was relentless, painting her life as chaotic and tumultuous. Cher deflected with humor, telling reporters, "The sad part of my life is that I don't have to do anything to have people think I'm doing too much."

Amid the chaos, Sonny Bono proved a surprising ally. When Cher sought his advice, he suggested she appear with him on *The Tonight Show* to deflect the media. Their banter charmed the audience and momentarily quelled the scrutiny. Cher also attended the Rock Music Awards, sharing the stage with Elton John and Diana Ross in an over-the-top entrance that reminded everyone of her star power.

Then came an unexpected call from Gregory's doctors in Buffalo, where he had checked into rehab. They praised his determination to recover and urged Cher to visit, believing her presence could aid his progress. Leaving Chas with Sonny, she joined Gregory in rehab. Together, they attended therapy, picked apples, and shared quiet moments watching movies. Gregory admitted feeling crushed under the weight of being "Mr. Cher" and despised the constant paparazzi attention. His vulnerability and sensitivity moved her, but Cher remained wary, knowing his world of music often invited relapse.

Despite her doubts, Cher chose to give Gregory another chance, dropping the divorce proceedings. Their love, though fragile, still held hope.

CHAPTER 18

TROUBLE IN PARADISE

Gregory invited Cher to Jamaica for a belated honeymoon, and as they prepared to leave, she noticed him packing a locked metal box. Curious, she asked, "What's in the box?" Gregory admitted it was methadone but insisted, "I don't need it," before dumping the bottles into the toilet. Cher, unsure what methadone was, didn't protest but sensed unease.

They arrived at Negril, a beautiful beach resort, and for a few days, life felt idyllic. Cher swam and soaked in the sun while an older woman from a nearby cottage cared for them. Gregory started calm but soon grew restless, which Cher recognized as a warning sign. One afternoon, she returned from the beach to find two strangers drinking rum with him. Gregory didn't introduce them, and Cher felt the tension building.

In the kitchen, she confided in the older woman, but Gregory burst in, loud and intimidating. Though Gregory wasn't violent, his size and demeanor were threatening. The woman pulled a knife and warned, "If you touch the little lady, I'll use this!" Gregory retreated, deflated by her fierce determination.

Later, with the woman's help, Cher packed her belongings and fled. As they left the cottage, they passed men chasing crabs along the beach with torches and sacks. A driver took Cher to Montego Bay, where she checked into a hotel, only to face another bizarre encounter–a waiter delivering a chocolate malt abruptly kissed her. Exhausted and shaken, Cher thought, *What a nightmare.* Her romantic getaway had turned into chaos.

The day after leaving Jamaica, Cher flew to Atlanta to meet Paulette. Plans to return to Los Angeles were interrupted when the Allman Brothers' roadies showed up, bringing her to a Jimmy Carter campaign event where the band was performing. Gregory joined them after a chaotic trip to Kingston, visibly shaken from his drug-seeking misadventures. Paulette, meanwhile, began dating Dickey Betts after his persistent efforts.

THE RETURN OF SONNY & CHER

Back in Los Angeles, Cher resumed rehearsals for the second season of her show. A summer hiatus had seen CBS replace her time slot with *Joey and Dad,* which flopped, losing viewers to *The Six Million Dollar*

Man. Despite a strong return, Cher's show struggled to reclaim its audience.

One day, a security guard at CBS asked Cher for ID at the studio entrance. Playfully, she returned the next day with a publicity photo pinned to her chest, amusing everyone and ending the rule for her. Despite setbacks, Cher cherished CBS, calling it a close-knit, supportive environment.

The second season faced challenges. Without David's influence, securing A-list guests became difficult. Still, Cher managed iconic collaborations, like singing "Georgia on My Mind" with Ray Charles and inviting David Bowie, who charmed her with his charisma and quirky Sears-bought outfit. Tina Turner's visit was more poignant. Before filming, Tina confided in Cher, asking how she left Sonny, hinting at her own troubled marriage with Ike. Cher's simple reply was, "I just walked out and kept going".

During this tumult, she ran into David Geffen, who raved about a self-actualization workshop called est. Intrigued, Cher persuaded Gregory to join her for the program, which quickly turned into an ordeal. With strict rules, public criticism, and long hours, the sessions felt like torment. Gregory fled after the first night, leaving Cher alone to face the emotional roller coaster. A man from the audience unexpectedly confronted her, blaming her for his divorce because his wife idolized Sonny and Cher. The awkward moment, paired with Gregory's absence, left her shaken. Alone in the bathroom, Cher realized she was pregnant.

Feeling overwhelmed, she turned to Sonny for support. They sat in their old bedroom as Cher confessed her struggles at work. "So you wanna work with me again?" she asked, to which Sonny instantly agreed with a laugh. Together, they pitched the idea of reviving *The Sonny & Cher Show* to CBS. The network agreed, reuniting the iconic duo for a historic comeback.

Despite her professional triumph, Cher faced personal challenges. She hadn't told Gregory about the pregnancy, but she mustered the courage to inform Sonny. "Son, I have to tell you something. I'm pregnant," she admitted. Sonny, though shocked, processed the news and quipped, "Cher, only you."

Sonny's focus shifted to damage control, navigating CBS's hesitations about Cher's pregnancy by Gregory Allman. Somehow, he managed to finalize the deal. Their reunion was nothing short of extraordinary–a divorced couple returning to prime-time television, with Cher carrying the child of her rock-star husband who had filed for divorce nine days after their wedding.

In December, the network announced *The Sonny & Cher Show* would return in February 1976. It marked a daring new beginning for the iconic pair, blending the surreal drama of their personal lives with their unmatched chemistry on stage.

Cher's second pregnancy coincided with the revival of *The Sonny & Cher Comedy Hour.* Knowing the baby was due three months after the first season's finale, Cher was determined to make it work. Trusting Bob Mackie to design costumes that would downplay her growing bump, she quipped, "I was their punishment," referencing the censors who had long tried to rein her in.

When Cher told Gregory about the pregnancy, he didn't believe her at first. Though he returned to Los Angeles briefly, the tabloids spun a narrative about her reunion with Sonny, painting Gregory as the outsider. The pressure broke him. In a heartfelt note, he wrote, "I almost wish I could live with being a fool, for then I could live with you." Then, he left.

Cher threw herself into work. At the Beverly Wilshire press conference announcing the show's return, Sonny fielded questions while Cher, unconcerned by skeptics, focused on their audience. "Getting to do *The Sonny & Cher Comedy Hour* again was a gift from heaven," she reflected.

On February 1, 1976, they made their triumphant return. Introduced as "together again for the first time," they received a standing ovation. Their playful banter quickly reignited their chemistry. Sonny teased Cher about her pregnancy, and she quipped back with ease, their humor sharper than ever. Performing "Love Will Keep Us Together," they reminded viewers why they had fallen in love with Sonny & Cher in the first place.

Though divorced, their comedic timing was unmatched. Memorable moments, like Sonny's repeated flubs while introducing Raymond Burr, showcased their infectious laughter and camaraderie. When Sonny's uncontrollable giggles set Cher off, the blooper reel became one of the season's highlights.

The show's success reaffirmed their unique bond. Despite the changes in their personal lives, they proved that their connection–rooted in humor, support, and mutual respect–remained unshakable. The audience still loved them, and they still had each other.

Meanwhile, Cher fulfilled her contractual obligations with Warner Bros., recording *I'd Rather Believe in You*. Despite her passion for singing, she struggled to connect with the album. Unlike *Stars*, her previous collaboration with Jimmy Webb, this project lacked her enthusiasm. Reflecting on her voice, Cher admitted she didn't appreciate it fully until years later when vocal coach Adrienne Angel transformed her perspective.

By the final episode of *The Sonny & Cher Comedy Hour*'s first season, Cher was six months pregnant. Diahann Carroll guest-starred, and the two performed a sailor-themed tap routine.

MONSTERS, MUSIC, AND MEMORIES

In March, Cher threw a monster-themed seventh birthday party for Chas, who adored *Young Frankenstein* and Gene Wilder. Chas, dressed as a boy with her father Sonny's distinct gait, watched the film with party guests. Cher recalled Chas's childhood love for Wilder, sparked by *Willy Wonka*, and how, years earlier, Gene had charmed her daughter by taking her for a stroll through Beverly Hills. At the party, Cher reflected on Chas's resilience through divorce, remarriage, and the media frenzy surrounding their lives. Despite everything, Chas was thrilled about her baby sibling and her parents' professional reunion, secretly hoping they'd reconcile.

Exhausted after late-night rehearsals, Cher looked forward to her Hawaii getaway with Chas and her trainer, Ange. In Kahala, Cher embraced the tranquility of beach life, kite-flying, and simple moments with Chas. Their outings included fending off overly helpful men attempting to "improve" their kite-flying skills. With humor, Cher learned to wave them off, enjoying the independence and joy of their time together. Strolling back from the beach one day, Cher overheard wolf whistles and turned to reveal her pregnant belly, reveling in the startled reactions of the admirers.

For Cher, Hawaii was a precious respite, a time to bond with Chas, reflect, and prepare for the changes ahead.

Before leaving for Hawaii, Cher gave Gregory an ultimatum: call her from rehab at Silver Hill psychiatric hospital by a set date in June or never call again. Exhausted by their repeated patterns, she told him, "I'm so tired of doing this." Gregory's soft reply, "But I keep going," struck her deeply, and she held onto hope. When the phone rang in Hawaii, Cher was thrilled to hear Gregory had made it to rehab. Yet the adrenaline rush of their conversation triggered premature contractions, sending her to Queen Kapi'olani Hospital.

Doctors administered an alcohol drip to relax her uterus, a terrifying experience for someone who didn't drink. Ange, Cher's trainer and friend, supported her, even washing her long hair in the hospital with a trash can as a makeshift sink.

When Gregory arrived, he took care of Chas and Cher, and the family spent five idyllic weeks in their rented oceanfront home. Cher rekindled her love for Gregory, but outside, tensions simmered. At a restaurant, a woman insulted Cher, mistaking her for a local islander. Later, a man punched Gregory, assuming the same. Disturbed, the couple decided to stay home, bonding over beachside meals with Chas.

Cher's assistant Paulette, in love with Dickey Betts, left to move to Sarasota, ending their partnership with an emotional goodbye. When it was time to return to LA, Cher's gynecologist accompanied them on the flight, ensuring her safety. Back home, her due date came and went. Still dilated but without labor, Cher realized she hadn't prepared the nursery. In a panic, she rushed to a baby boutique, shocking saleswomen as she announced she was five centimeters dilated.

Finally, on July 10, Cher was induced. Gregory stayed by her side, emotional as their son, Elijah Skye Blue, was born–a healthy seven pounds, six ounces, with blond hair and eyelashes just like his father. Cher chose his middle names after the blue skies she'd gazed at in Hawaii, fighting to keep him.

Back at home, the family's bliss grew as Elijah's big sister Chas doted on him. One night, Cher discovered Chas casually carrying the baby down the hall, a habit she'd secretly developed. Though alarmed, Cher simply suggested they hold him together next time. Their family, though imperfect, was finding its rhythm amidst the chaos.

CHAPTER 19

A NIGHT AT THE WHITE HOUSE

In January 1977, Jimmy Carter, a peanut farmer from Georgia, became the thirty-ninth president of the United States. Gregory and Cher attended his first cocktail party at the White House, a gesture of gratitude to the "Georgia Peanut Brigade," Carter's dedicated supporters.

As the evening wound down, Cher asked to see the Mary Todd Lincoln table setting. The porcelain dinnerware, commissioned by Lincoln's wife, amazed her with its intricate design of purple and gold scalloped edges and the iconic American eagle. As a longtime admirer of Abraham Lincoln, seeing these historical pieces thrilled her. Their tour extended to the personal quarters, where they marveled at first ladies' artifacts, the "Nixon piano," and even the Lincoln Bedroom, once Lincoln's office. Caught up in the moment, Cher playfully flopped onto the high, narrow bed and danced around, drawing laughter from everyone, including Gregory and Miss Lillian, Carter's vivacious seventy-eight-year-old mother.

Miss Lillian entertained Gregory with her sharp wit while Cher explored the bathroom, noticing a bottle of Wild Turkey bourbon. "I brought it from Georgia as a precaution," Miss Lillian explained. "Who knows what kind of liquor they have up here?"

Suddenly, nine-year-old Amy Carter burst in with an invitation: "Mama wants y'all to stay for dinner." They accepted eagerly. The private family dinner, featuring smothered chicken, black-eyed peas, and cornbread, felt intimate and warm. Jimmy shared his vision to create jobs for Americans, his genuine passion and honesty filling the room with hope. The family's humility, from their simple meal to their lack of pretension, endeared them to everyone, including the White House staff.

After dinner, the group gathered for photos. Among them was Joe D, Cher's guest with a criminal past, which made her nervous. Her unease eased when Jimmy revealed that Mary, Amy's nanny, had been wrongly imprisoned before Rosalynn and Jimmy helped clear her name.

As they left, Gregory beamed with pride, knowing he had contributed to Carter's campaign. "It was the Allman Brothers that put me in the White House," Carter later declared. Cher, equally proud, marveled at the surreal night where history and humanity intertwined.

By 1977, life had settled into a rhythm for Cher and Gregory. They had moved to a three-bedroom Spanish-style house on Linden Drive in Beverly Hills, leaving behind the sprawling mansion where Elijah was born. Cher reminisced about the lavish home and Chas's over-the-top pink bedroom, but she laughed when Chas confessed, "Mom, I have to tell you something . . . I hate pink."

A YEAR OF CHANGE AND REFLECTION

In March, Sonny and Cher gave what would likely be their final performances on *The Sonny & Cher Comedy Hour*. For one memorable show, they recreated their 1964 look, complete with bobcat vests and Sonny's Prince Valiant wig. Together, they sang "Baby Don't Go," the first song they recorded as a duo. When their TV option wasn't renewed, they were disappointed but proud of their groundbreaking show. Cher found solace in Fred Silverman's words, calling it "a monumental hit."

That summer, they embarked on a reunion tour, taking Chas and Elijah along. Sonny, always great with the kids, captured Elijah crawling in hotel hallways. Back home, Cher occasionally visited Sonny in Palm Springs, where he hosted barbecues and reflected on his past mistakes. One day, he arrived at Cher's doorstep in tears, apologizing for how his infidelity had hurt her and others. Cher appreciated his honesty, even though it couldn't undo the past.

Gregory spent much of the year on tour with his new band, the Gregg Allman Band. Together, Gregory and Cher released *Two the Hard Way* under the name "Allman and Woman." Cher loved collaborating with him in the studio, especially on "Do What You Gotta Do," a song that resonated deeply with their relationship. Despite their efforts, the album didn't meet her expectations.

Later that summer, Cher, Gregory, and Chas traveled to Japan for Gregory's tour. The trip was a cultural adventure, with Gregory towering over the locals and Chas charming shopkeepers. One man even offered Cher $500 for her jeans, which she proudly refused. After Japan, they went to Europe, but their time there unraveled when Cher discovered Gregory was secretly drinking. Heartbroken, she packed her bags and flew home.

In late 1977, Cher and Sonny flew to Hawaii for their final mini-tour. Rehearsals took an unexpected turn when Cher spotted a familiar figure–her ex, Bill–standing with his guitar. Sonny, ever the schemer, had orchestrated this to unsettle her. Cher was initially shocked but couldn't help laughing at Sonny's audacity. However, the plan backfired when Cher and Bill reconnected during the tour. Though brief, their time together rekindled old feelings, adding an unexpected twist to the trip. Their last performance, on New Year's Eve at the Hilton Hawaiian Village, ended with a poignant rendition of *"I Got You Babe."*

Cher had long dreamed of performing *West Side Story* in its entirety, a passion dating back to her teenage years. Finally, for her ABC special, she fulfilled that dream, playing all ten characters with the magic of chroma-key technology. Art Fisher directed, and Cher seamlessly transformed into Maria, Anita, the Jets, and the Sharks, creating a visual and emotional spectacle. "It felt magical," she later reflected. The special also included her family, with Chas and Elijah helping her recreate moments from her childhood, adding a personal touch to the production. The show closed with her singing *"A Dream Is a Wish Your Heart Makes"* as Elijah hilariously botched a planned moment, adding unscripted charm.

DREAMS, NEW FACES, AND NEW BEGINNINGS

Back in Beverly Hills, Cher embraced life with her two children. Elijah, now 18 months old, was a lively toddler, and Chas adored her little brother, often playing by the pool or at the beach with him. Gregory visited during his periods of sobriety, creating precious moments with Elijah at the piano. Yet trouble lingered. Chas once confided that Gregory had taken her to a bar after school, prompting Cher to confront her growing fears.

Gregory's paranoia reached a breaking point when he hallucinated men with guns in their backyard. For Cher, this was the last straw. She realized it was no longer safe for her children. Despite her deep love for Gregory, their relationship had become unsustainable. They divorced in early 1978, marking the end of a tumultuous chapter.

Cher threw herself into work, filming a new ABC special slated for April. She expanded her creative role, co-producing and writing for the show. Her guests included Rod Stewart, the Tubes, and Dolly Parton, who embodied "good" opposite the Tubes' "evil." Cher had met Dolly at a party, instantly drawn to her unique style and charm. Their friendship blossomed, and Dolly's appearance became a highlight of the special.

Not long after, Cher found herself at a reception hosted by Neil Bogart, where she had a comical misunderstanding about meeting Gene Simmons of Kiss, mistaking him for the actress Jean Simmons. Despite her initial embarrassment, Cher and Gene struck up a surprising connection. Beneath the Demon persona, she discovered a thoughtful, sober man devoted to his mother, a Holocaust survivor. Though their first date ended poorly, Gene's persistence and heartfelt gestures, including showering Chas with Kiss merchandise, won Cher over. They began an unexpected but pleasant relationship.

As Cher's personal life took new turns, she decided to create a lasting sanctuary for herself and her children. She purchased a four-acre plot in Benedict Canyon, envisioning an Egyptian-inspired home where they could find peace and privacy. The land, previously owned by a Disney cel painter, offered a blank slate for her dreams. Her fascination with Egyptian culture–its architecture, art, and mystique–shaped her plans for the home, promising a unique space that reflected her creativity and individuality.

Balancing her work, family, and budding romance, Cher continued to navigate life's complexities with resilience, humor, and an unwavering sense of self. Whether fulfilling childhood dreams or building a future for her family, she embraced each moment with determination and grace.

BUILDING DREAMS AND FINDING BALANCE

The six-bedroom property Cher envisioned as "the Egyptian house" was inspired by ancient North African designs, with whitewashed walls and ornate iron details. Its most striking feature was a glass roof over a central courtyard that electronically opened to the sky, alongside narrow, dramatic floor-to-ceiling windows. Architect Ted Grenzbach, known for traditional styles, was initially hesitant about the unconventional project but embraced Cher's vision after reviewing her sketches from *Jesus of Nazareth*. Construction was lengthy and costly, but bit by bit, her dream home began to take shape.

During this time, Gene Simmons, Cher's new romantic interest, rented a bungalow at the Beverly Hills Hotel to spend more time with her. Cher, cautious about relationships, took things slowly. "I don't want to wake up next to someone I can't talk to," she explained. Gene patiently respected her boundaries, impressing her with thoughtful gestures like writing "I Love You Cher" in the sky for her birthday. The day's festivities included a marching band, a tank filled with Snickers bars, and a celebration at Le Dome restaurant.

Gene's connection with Cher's children deepened their bond. He showered Chas and Elijah with attention, teaching Elijah to swim, giving him his first guitar, and taking Chas to the movies. Chas even contributed to Gene's solo single *"Living in Sin,"* fulfilling her dreams as a Kiss fan. Gene also set Cher's sister up with his bandmate Paul Stanley, making them a close-knit group of travelers.

However, Gene struggled with the spotlight in Los Angeles. Dating Cher blurred his carefully maintained boundary between his public and private personas. Though they navigated press intrusion, Gene remained attentive, even inviting Cher and the kids to join him in England while recording an album. In the countryside, they bonded over soccer games, giant dogs, and laughter, with Elijah endearingly calling their bodyguard "Eddie Bananas."

Despite his rock-star persona, Gene's sweetness shone through. Cher once slapped him playfully when he tried to act as his stage persona, "the Demon." "I'm not putting up with that!" she warned, and Gene quickly returned to his loving self. Their time together revealed a balance of fun, family, and affection, with Gene cherishing his role in Cher's life and her children's.

CHAPTER 20

A NEW ERA

In 1978, Cher decided to explore her musical range and record a rock album. However, her record label head, Neil Bogart, persuaded her to try disco first, assuring her it was the hottest trend. Despite initial doubts, she trusted Neil's judgment and recorded *Take Me Home*, produced by Bob Esty. When the title track played back in the studio, everyone sensed it was a hit. Their instincts proved right: the album soared to number eight on the Billboard charts, staying there for five months. Gene Simmons conceptualized the album cover, featuring Cher in a dazzling gold bikini with wings and a dramatic headdress. "I looked like a barmaid from Valhalla," she quipped.

Acting had been Cher's dream since childhood, a passion nurtured by performing *West Side Story* solo in her living room. Despite her success on *The Sonny & Cher Comedy Hour* and an Emmy, Hollywood refused to take her seriously. "You're not the kind I need," Mike Nichols told her bluntly when she auditioned for *The Fortune*. Undeterred, Cher boldly declared, "I'm really talented, and one day you'll be sorry," before storming out. Other encounters were far less professional–like a disturbing meeting with producer Ray Stark that left her running for the door. Her attempts to secure film roles proved fruitless, and Cher had no choice but to return to what she knew: performing live.

Preparing for her first solo tour without Sonny, Cher knew the show had to be spectacular. Producer Joe Layton brought an elaborate concept, featuring drag performers as Cher, Bette Midler, and Diana Ross. The impersonators were so convincing that even friends of Bette and Diana were fooled backstage. Cher found her own double, Elgin Kenna, who was so uncanny she sometimes felt like she was looking in a mirror.

The tour debuted at the Sahara in Reno in 1979. Backstage, Cher battled crippling stage fright. Without Sonny to push her onstage, she looked at herself in the mirror, doubting her decision. "You're never going to be able to do this," she thought. Her new assistant, Deb Paull, who had no experience in show business, tried to steady her nerves. Deb's arrival into Cher's world had been almost comedic–she'd driven from Ohio with melted vinyl records in her car–but her enthusiasm and loyalty made her indispensable. Decades later, Deb remained one of Cher's most trusted confidantes.

The opening night began with a twist: instead of a dazzling gown, Cher emerged as her scrappy, comedic alter ego, Laverne. Tottering through the audience, muttering in her thick Brooklyn accent, she immediately broke the ice. As the crowd roared with laughter, she slipped backstage for a quick change into a Bob Mackie masterpiece. But the performance was plagued with technical issues—a fire alarm, a malfunctioning mic. Quick on her feet, Cher quipped, “I know I’m hot, but this is crazy,” drawing laughter from the crowd. When her mic cut out again, she joked, “I knew Sonny was going to come here and screw this up!” The audience’s laughter confirmed what she needed to hear: she could succeed on her own.

VEGAS AND BEYOND

Following the success of her solo show, Cher embarked on her first residency at Caesars Palace in Las Vegas, extending her performances to Lake Tahoe, Atlantic City, and Washington, D.C. Critics dismissed her as a sellout, but Cher remained unfazed, breaking Frank Sinatra’s attendance record in her first month. “People loved the show,” she said, brushing off skeptics. “I’ll still be here after they’re gone,” she confidently told one relentless critic.

Her *Take Me Home* residency was a spectacle unlike anything audiences had seen before. Cher’s dynamic act featured dazzling Bob Mackie costumes, wild props, and a brilliant cast, including drag impersonators of Cher, Bette Midler, and Diana Ross. Michael Keaton opened the show with his sharp comedy, while Cher transformed into a succession of stunning looks, sticking to her rule of never wearing the same outfit for more than ten minutes. With backdrops of home videos of Chas and Elijah and a voiceover from her mother joking, “She always did want to be naked,” Cher’s performances mixed humor, glamour, and heart.

Despite the grueling schedule of two shows a night, Cher and her team found time to bond. After each performance, they’d unwind at Cleopatra’s Barge or dance until dawn at all-night clubs, often emerging into the blinding morning sunlight. Cher’s close-knit crew became her second family, making the later toll of AIDS on her dancers and friends particularly devastating. “I went to so many bedside farewells,” she recalled, mourning the loss of vibrant performers like Kenny Sacha and Michael Perea.

The residency’s success led Cher to the Kennedy Center Opera House in Washington, D.C., an experience marked by an unsettling revelation. During rehearsals, she noticed heightened security but brushed it off until a teenage boy tried to jump on stage during her performance. The FBI’s aggressive response seemed excessive, prompting Cher to question her agent. Finally, her agent admitted the truth: a death threat had been made against her. The FBI shadowed her every move, even as she evaded them for a brief shopping trip. Reflecting on the incident, Cher shrugged, "Well, I guess they missed their chance."

Even with these challenges, Cher's Vegas chapter solidified her as an unparalleled performer. The glittering shows, the camaraderie with her crew, and her resilience through personal and professional obstacles all underscored her tenacity. The stage, as ever, was where Cher shined brightest, proving to critics and fans alike that she was here to stay.

DREAMS IN PROGRESS

Meanwhile, Cher's personal life was evolving. She supported her mother, Georgia, who opened a store called Granny's Cabbage Patch in Brentwood. It was there Georgia met Craig Spencer, a man a year younger than Cher. What began as a potential match for Cher's sister Gee turned into a romance for Georgia herself. Though the store struggled financially, Georgia found happiness with Craig, and over time, Cher and Craig became close friends.

Cher moved with Chas and Elijah to a cozy home in Malibu Colony, complete with a pool and tennis court. Elijah adored his sister, calling her "Da" after a hilarious attempt to pronounce "Chastity." He was spirited and mischievous, earning the nickname "General Fatface" as a baby. Cher fondly recalled chasing after him during his muddy adventures, marveling at his stubborn determination, which reminded her of her own childhood.

Chas, mature for her age, leaned toward tomboyish attire and a responsible demeanor. But a school principal's harsh claim that Chas had emotional issues deeply upset Cher. Thankfully, Chas's teacher, Betsy Glaser, encouraged Cher to have her tested for dyslexia. Specialists confirmed the diagnosis, explaining Chas's academic struggles. Reading about dyslexia, Cher had a startling realization: *That's me.* Testing for dyslexia hadn't existed during her childhood, but the discovery brought clarity to her past challenges and allowed her to provide Chas with the support she never had.

That Christmas, Cher headed to Aspen with her family–Pauli, Gee, Chas, and three-year-old Elijah. They rented a cozy condo, later replaced by their beloved log cabin with its towering fireplace. It became the setting for festive traditions: home-cooked meals, decorating sessions, and a fiercely competitive annual Christmas cookie contest that Cher always won. The cabin even had a room above the kitchen for Pauli, accessible only by a ladder Cher playfully locked her in on occasion. Elijah, discovering snow for the first time in a blizzard, frowned and asked, “What the hell is this?” Despite his youth, Cher fibbed about his age to enroll him in ski lessons. He quickly became a fearless skier, following in Chas’s tracks.

By early 1980, Cher was back on the road, performing worldwide. While she and Gene Simmons remained friends, their relationship ended, and Cher channeled her focus into her career and family. She finally moved into her dream Egyptian house, which had cost a fortune to build and contributed to her financial troubles. Between overspending and paying Sonny $1.4 million to settle an old contract, Cher found herself on the brink of Chapter 11. Sitting at the kitchen table, staring at the papers, she felt defeated. Then her business manager delivered a miracle: a real estate buyer paid her in full, saving her from financial ruin. Relieved, she vowed to be more cautious—but as she admitted, “I’ve been overextending myself my whole life.”

Cher threw lively Sunday barbecues at her new house, cooking dishes like her famous tomato-olive-potato salad. The home buzzed with joy, though not without drama. One day, Elijah, thrilled with his drivable toy car from Santa, sped down the long driveway as Cher arrived in her Jeep. Swerving to avoid him, she thought she’d run him over. Shaken, she found him unharmed and scolded her staff for not watching him. That night, they went to see *Mommie Dearest*, a choice Cher later joked about given her fiery temper earlier that day.

Cher’s unconventional life meant her children joined her on tour, loving the adventure of late nights, swimming pools, and hotel antics. She even brought them to South Africa and Australia, ensuring tutors accompanied them when necessary. During her *Black Rose* tour, Cher briefly dated guitarist Les Dudek, a kind and humorous musician known for his work with the Allman Brothers and Steve Miller Band.

Amid her thriving music career, Cher couldn’t shake her childhood dream of becoming a serious actress. Despite an Emmy-winning TV career and worldwide fame, Hollywood dismissed her as “too old, too ethnic, or too typecast.” Even Jack Nicholson’s introduction to director Mike Nichols resulted in rejection. “You’re not the kind of woman I need for this role,” Nichols had said, prompting Cher to boldly declare, “One day, you’re going to be sorry.”

The turning point came during her Las Vegas residency. Backstage at Caesars Palace, Cher was surprised by an old friend: Francis Ford Coppola. With four Oscars under his belt, Coppola praised her performance and asked, "Why aren't you making movies?" Fighting back tears, Cher explained the industry's rejection. Coppola offered her a challenge: "Until you do something, nobody will believe you can. The worst that can happen is you fail—but at least you'll have tried."

His words reignited Cher's determination. Shelley Winters' earlier advice echoed in her mind: "If you're serious about acting, stop messing around and go to New York." As Coppola smiled and asked, "What are you waiting for?"